D. H Lovell

Practical Switch Work

A Handbook for Track Foremen

D. H Lovell

Practical Switch Work
A Handbook for Track Foremen

ISBN/EAN: 9783337106546

Printed in Europe, USA, Canada, Australia, Japan

Cover: Foto ©ninafisch / pixelio.de

More available books at **www.hansebooks.com**

INDEX.

PREFACE.

THERE is, perhaps, no part of track work in regard to which there are so many unimportant differences of opinion upon the part of trackmen as that which pertains to switch work. Trackmen naturally form their opinions from local conditions, and follow the practices of their predecessors or the instructions of their superiors, so it would be only natural for each one to think that his way is the best.

This book is intended for the trackman particularly, to give him, in a concise and comprehensive way, what is the best general track practice, from which he may select that which will best meet the requirements or conditions under which he may work.

There are, of necessity, in a book of this kind slight but unimportant departures from mathematical accuracy, also what may seem unnecessary detail of explanation, and also the use and frequent repetition of words or expressions which are common among trackmen, all of which are necessary to make it thoroughly understood and useful to this most worthy class of practical men.

It is not expected that the formulas will be intelligible to them, but, so far as possible, where it is necessary, the formula is accompanied by a simple mathematical demonstration, which, it is hoped, will not be beyond the clear understanding of all.

It is not claimed that this is something new and superior to anything hitherto published.

It is simply a combination of theory and practice, so far as possible, based upon common sense in track work and verified in the experience of hundreds of the best trackmen of the day. So there need be no hesitation to use what is in the book from a fear that it may not be correct, should it happen not to be in strict accord with local practices.

THE TURNOUT.

The single turnout from one track to another is the most simple of all switch connections, the more complicated ones being only developments of it, and what is true of it is also true of them.

The turnout curve, from a theoretical point of view, is most generally assumed to be a simple circular arc or curve, beginning at the point of the switch point or head-block, as C, and ending at the point of the frog B, as shown in diagram No. 1 :—

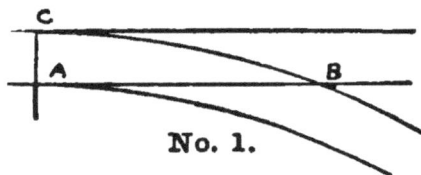

No. 1.

That portion of the turnout between the head-block and the frog point, as A to B, is called the lead, and its length for a point, or split switch, as it is most generally called, is the distance from the point of the turnout curve or, in this case, the head-block of the split switch, to the point of the frog measured along the main or straight rail, as A to B in diagram No. 1 ; and for a stub switch it is the distance to the frog

point from the head-block only, the former being called the "point lead" and the latter the
"stub lead."

The turnout curve is from C to B, and although the difference in distance between it and
the lead from A to B is only a few inches, it
should not be mistaken for the lead, nor so regarded.

Whether the turnout is from a straight or
curved track, or the switch is a point or a stub,
the lead should be measured, as from A to B,
along the main rail in which the frog is already
or is to be placed.

Before any lead can be calculated or ascertained it is necessary to know the gauge of the
track, the frog number, and, in the case of a stub
switch, the throw also, as the lead and the degree of the turnout curve vary for every different frog, throw, and gauge.

Practically, the difference of a half inch between the two standard gauges—4 feet 8½ and
4 feet 9 inches—is so small that there need
be no difference between them recognized, although it is well to do so where the distances or
rules for each gauge are given to calculate the
lead.

The "throw" is the distance the sliding or
moving rails move at the head-block.   The

throw of a point switch in nowise affects the lead, but the throw of a stub switch does.

It has been found in practice that the theoretical length of the lead as obtained upon the assumption that the curve begins at the point of the switch and ends at the point of the frog, is too long when used for frogs higher than No. 7, and makes the turnout curve flat near the switch or sharp, in comparison, near the frog. This is on account of the switch point not being thin enough to conform to the theoretical curve, its gauge line at the heel being several inches inside the theoretical curve at that point.

To remedy this it is the practice to reduce the length of the lead so as to obtain a more uniform turnout curve between the heel of the switch and the frog point.

To distinguish these two leads, one is called the "theoretical" or long lead, and the other the "practical" or short lead.

THE THEORETICAL LEAD.

As has been mentioned before, the theoretical lead is the distance to the frog point obtained by calculation upon the assumption that the turnout curve begins at the switch point and ends at the frog point.

For the engineer, the formula or mathematics for this lead, for any gauge and frog, is $l = 2gn$, in which l is the lead, g the gauge, and n the frog number.

For the trackman, it means that the lead is equal to twice the gauge multiplied by the frog number.

For example: What is the lead of a No. 10 frog, 4 feet 9 inch gauge? Twice 4 feet 9 inches is equal to 9 feet 6 inches, or $9\frac{1}{2}$ feet, and ten times $9\frac{1}{2}$ feet are 95 feet, which is the theoretical or full lead of a No. 10 frog, 4 feet 9 inch gauge.

For the same frog and 4 feet $8\frac{1}{2}$ inch gauge, the lead is twice 4 feet $8\frac{1}{2}$ inches, or 9 feet 5 inches, which, multiplied by 10, equals 94 feet 2 inches.

For No. 8 frog and 4 feet 9 inch gauge, it is 76 feet; and for 4 feet $8\frac{1}{2}$ inch gauge, it is 75 feet 4 inches.

It is evident from this that the one-half inch difference between these two standard gauges is so small as not to affect the lead practically, and it is not necessary to make any distinction between them in considering and applying practical rules. But for the purpose of making this formula and rule more easily remembered and useful to the trackman, it can be simplified in this way :

Rule.—For 4 feet 8½ inch and 4 feet 9 inch gauges, the theoretical or long lead is equal, practically, to 9½ times the frog number.

9½ times 10 equals 95 feet, the lead for No. 10 frog.
9½ times 8 equals 76 feet, " " 8 "
9½ times 6 equals 57 feet, " " 6 "

This will not apply to any other than 4 feet 8½ inch and 4 feet 9 inch gauges, and with point or split switches. For all other gauges use the rule of "twice the gauge multiplied by the frog number" for the theoretical lead.

The following is a table of leads obtained by this rule for 3 feet, 4 feet 8½, and 4 feet 9 inch gauges :—

TABLE No. 1.

THEORETICAL LEADS.

FROG No.	LEADS.				
	4 Feet 8½ inches.		4 Feet 9 inches.		3 Feet.
	Feet.	Inches.	Feet.	Inches.	Feet.
4	37	8	38	0	24
5	47	1	47	6	30
6	56	6	57	0	36
7	65	11	66	6	42
8	75	4	76	0	48
9	84	9	85	6	54
10	94	2	95	0	60
11	103	7	104	6	
12	113	0	114	0	
15	141	3	142	6	

The use of this table is very simple. Having decided upon the number of the frog to be used in the turnout, refer to the table, and opposite the frog number will be found the theoretical lead. Place the frog that distance from the head-block of the point or split switch.

If, however, a shorter lead is desired, refer to Table No. 3, on page 16, in which are given shortened leads, which may be used instead.

The choice between the theoretical and the shortened lead is optional; either is good enough, but the shortened one will give a better line to the turnout curve, and is therefore preferable.

TABLE No. 2.

CORRECT (NOT APPROXIMATE) FROG ANGLES, DEGREES, RADII, AND POINT LEADS.

No.	Frog Angle		Degree of Curve				Radius		Theoretical Point Lead				Short Lead	
	4 Ft. 8½ In.		4 Ft. 8½ In.		4 Ft. 9 In.		4 Ft. 8½ In.	4 Ft. 9 In.	4 Ft. 8½ In.		4 Ft. 9 In.			
	Angle °	′	°	′	°	′	Feet	Feet	Ft.	In.	Ft.	In.	Ft.	In.
4	14	15	38	46	38	24½	150.66	152.0	37	8	38	0	38	0
5	11	25	24	32	24	18½	235.40	237.5	47	1	47	6	47	6
6	9	32	16	58	16	48½	338.98	342.0	56	6	57	0	57	0
7	8	10	12	26½	12	20	461.38	465.5	65	11	66	6	66	6
8	7	09	9	31	9	26	602.62	608.0	75	4	76	0	72	0
9	6	22	7	31	7	27½	762.69	769.5	84	9	85	6	78	0
10	5	44	6	05½	6	02	941.60	950.0	94	2	95	0	85	0
11	5	12	5	02	4	59	1139.34	1149.5	103	7	104	6	90	0
12	4	46	4	13½	4	11	1355.90	1368.0	113	0	114	0	96	0
15	3	49	2	42	2	41	2188.85	2137.5	141	3	142	6	120	0
20	2	52	1	31	1	30½	3766.67	3800.0	188	4	190	0	130	0

This table is correct, the other tables giving only approximate figures.

THE SHORTENED, OR PRACTICAL, LEAD.

The practical lead differs from the theoretical lead in being shorter, and consequently improves the alignment of the turnout curve for frogs higher in number than seven.

The circumstances to be considered in determining how much the theoretical lead should be shortened are : the clearance necessary at the heel of the switch point as a flangeway for the passing wheel, the length of the switch point or point rails, and the economical use of material.

The clearance between the gauge line of the main rail and the outside of the head of the switch point at the heel should not be less than $2\frac{1}{2}$ nor more than $3\frac{1}{2}$ inches, 3 inches being preferable.

If this clearance is added to the width of the rail head, which is about $2\frac{1}{4}$ or $2\frac{1}{2}$ inches, the distance, gauge to gauge, at the heel of the switch point would be about 5 or $5\frac{1}{2}$ inches. Assuming that this distance corresponds to the throw of a stub switch, the stub lead can be calculated, giving a curve from the frog point to the heel of the switch point which would conform, between those points, to the theoretical curve when the lead is obtained by the rule of "twice the gauge," referred to on the preceding pages. And if to this stub lead, so obtained, the length of the switch point is added, provided it is not less than 15 nor more than 20 feet long, a good shortened lead for any frog can be obtained.

When any switch point less than 15 feet is used the clearance at the heel should be reduced slightly, otherwise the alignment from the heel to the point of the switch rail would make a too abrupt change in the turnout curve at that point.

But to properly secure the switch point at the heel with splices, the clearance should not be less than 3 inches, or about $5\frac{1}{2}$ inches, gauge to gauge. For that reason, about 15 feet is the least desirable length of switch point. A good rule for the shortened lead is as follows: For 4 feet $8\frac{1}{2}$ inch and 4 feet 9 inch gauges the lead for all frogs up to and including a No. 7 is $9\frac{1}{2}$ times the frog number; for No. 8, 9 times the number; for Nos. 9 and 10, $8\frac{1}{2}$ times the number; and for all from Nos. 10 to 15, 8 times the number of the frog.

The exceptions to this rule are that the lead for No. 9 may be 78 feet instead of 76 feet 6 inches, and for No. 11, 90 feet instead of 88 feet. However, those obtained by the rule are not too short.

TABLE No. 3.

SHORTENED LEADS.

FROG No.	TIMES THE FROG	SHORT LEAD.		THEORETICAL LEAD.	
		Feet.	Inches.	Feet.	Inches.
4	9½	38	0	38	0
5	9½	47	6	47	6
6	9½	57	0	57	0
7	9½	66	6	66	6
8	9	72	0	76	0
9	8½	76	6	85	6
10	8½	85	0	95	0
11	8	88	0	104	6
12	8	96	0	114	0
15	8	120	0	142	6

In this table, in the second column, are the number of times the frog number is to be multiplied to obtain the short lead, and in the third column are the short leads so obtained, the last column showing the theoretical leads for comparison.

It will be observed that the lead is not shortened for frogs less than No. 8, it not being necessary to do so, as the theoretical curve at the heel of the switch is more than 5 or 5½ inches from the gauge of the main rail for frogs less than No. 8.

In this consideration the shortened lead is obtained by moving the heel of the switch in the direction of the frog to the point on the turnout curve where the distance from the main rail to the theoretical curve is about equal to 5 or 5½ inches, the distance between the frog and the heel of the switch point corresponding to the stub lead for a throw of 5 or 5½ inches, the switch point, 15 or 18 feet long, being added to complete the short lead.

Although the shortened leads as here given are very good, it may be well to vary from them whenever it can be done without detriment to the efficiency of the turnout, in order to avoid a waste of rail by cutting, as what is given here as short leads is merely to show to what extent the theoretical lead can be safely reduced, for these short leads are not arbitrary ones which should not be varied from when it is better to do so. Any variation, however, will depend upon the length of the switch point or split switch, the distance from point to toe of frogs, and also upon what lengths of rail are available for the turnout.

The variety of distances from point to toe of frogs and different lengths of switch points make it difficult to even suggest any definite lengths of rail between the frog and switch to meet the requirements of various locations and conditions.

2

However, in the following table is an illustra-
tion of how the economical use of material can
be observed without varying much from the
shortened lead as given in Table No. 3, the
switch point in this case being 18 feet long and
frog from point to toe 7½ feet:

TABLE No. 4.

ADAPTING LEAD TO THE MATERIAL.

FROG No.	SHORT LEAD.	MATERIAL.			
		Switch.	Rails.	Frog.	Total Lead.
	Ft. In.	Feet.	Feet.	Ft. In.	Ft. In.
6	57 0	18	30	7 6	55 6
7	66 6	18	25 +15	7 6	65 6
8	72 0	18	30 +15	7 6	70 6
9	78 0	18	27½ +25	7 6	78 0
10	85 0	18	30 +30	7 6	85 6
11	90 0	18	50 +13½	7 6	89 0
12	96 0	18	60 +15	7 6	100 6
15	120 0	18	90	7 5	115 6

For a short lead for a No. 8 frog, which
would be about 72 feet long, use a rail 30 feet
long and cut one into two pieces 15 feet long.
Those pieces, making 45 feet, are all that are necessary between the switch and the frog, and
with the 18-foot switch point and 7½ feet from
point to toe of frog, make 70 feet 6 inches,
which is a good lead and can be used without

any hesitation. For No. 11 frog, two 25-foot rails and a 15-foot piece, making a lead of 90½ feet, is a preferable variation from 88 or 90 feet. The object should be to make but one cut to get two pieces to fill out.

So long as the lead of a No. 8 is not less than 69 or 70 feet it is very good, but it should not be less than 69 feet if it can be avoided.

If the switch point is 15 instead of 18 feet, then use two 25-foot rails, which would make the lead 72 feet 6 inches. Each case should determine to what extent the material can be adapted, it being permissible to vary a few feet either way from the shortened leads as given, but for a No. 8 frog it should not be more than 73 feet.

Instead of cutting the 30-foot rail exactly into two pieces 15 feet long, to be placed between the frog and switch, cut one 14 feet 11 inches and the other 15 feet 1 inch long, and place the longer piece in the curved and the shorter in the straight track. This will enable the heel of the switch points to be exactly opposite each other, and the joint ties will be square across the tracks.

All cases cannot, of course, be adapted to the material, owing to the difficulty to obtain rails of suitable length, but in shortening the lead the object should be to avoid a waste of material, and at the same time to adhere as closely as possible to the short leads given in Table No. 3.

For any short lead use the formula—

$$l = 2n \left(g - \sqrt{gt} \right)$$

and add the length of the switch point.

If the switch is less than 15 feet, say 10 or 12 feet, assume a throw less than 5 inches, but in no case less than 4 inches.

Note that in Table No. 4, adapting the lead to the material, the lead of Nos. 9 and 11 frogs has been increased.

TURNOUTS FROM CURVES.

The preceding pages have referred only to turnouts from a straight track.

It happens frequently that it is necessary to put in a turnout from a curve, and the first and very natural question is, whether the lead suitable for a turnout from a straight track will do also for one from a curve, no difference how sharp it is, or upon which side of the curve the turnout may be. The answer to this is that the same lead can be used whether the turnout is from a straight track or from a curve, as the lead, theoretically, when the turnout is from a curve, is only a few inches different in length from what it is when it is from a straight track.

Making the lead longer when the turnout is from the inside of a curve is generally resorted to for the purpose of reducing the curvature of the turnout, and, without reflection, it would seem to be the proper way to overcome the difficulty, but it does not do so unless a frog of higher number, which requires a longer lead, is used. A frog of higher number corresponding to the desired lead should be used, as the longer lead is for a frog of smaller angle, the remedy being in the frog of less angle and longer lead, and not in the increased lead without a different frog.

TURNOUTS FROM THE INSIDE OF CURVES.

When a turnout is from a curve, its curvature is greater or less than it would be from a straight track, according to whether it is from the inside or outside of the curve. If it is from the inside, it will be greater; if from the outside, it will be less than it would be from a straight track.

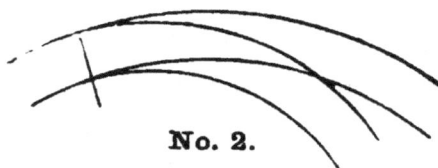

No. 2.

For example: a No. 8 frog in a straight track has for the turnout about a $9\frac{1}{2}$-degree curve. The same frog from the inside of a curve has for the turnout a curve equal to the degree of the main track curve added to $9\frac{1}{2}$, the degree of the curve for a No. 8 frog.

Suppose the main track curve is 4 degrees; by adding $9\frac{1}{2}$ degrees we have $13\frac{1}{2}$ degrees as the curvature of the turnout curve.

The turnout being from the inside of the 4-degree curve increases the curvature of the turnout from $9\frac{1}{2}$ to $13\frac{1}{2}$ degrees.

If the main-track curve should be 6 degrees, the turnout curve would be 15½ degrees, or 9½ added to 6 degrees.

Before making a connection from the inside of a curve, first ascertain what the degree of the main-track curve is. The method for doing this is given under the heading, "To Ascertain the Degree of Curvature."

Having ascertained the degree, then decide upon the number of the frog to be used or how sharp a turnout curve is desired.

To ascertain what is the degree of curvature through a frog upon a curve refer to Tables Nos. 5 and 6. Add the degree of the curve through the frog in a straight track to the degree of the curve of the track in which the frog is to be placed, and their sum will be equal to the degree of the turnout curve. If the sum of these two gives a curvature too great, then use a frog of a higher number to give the curvature desired.

Great care should be taken not to have a frog upon the inside of a curve that will make the turnout curve so sharp that it will always be a source of annoyance and expense from the track spreading or derailments.

There is a limit to the degree of curvature in turnouts. Ordinarily no frog should be placed upon the inside of a curve which will make the turnout curve greater than about 16 degrees, or that suitable to a No. 6 frog, unless engines especially adapted to very sharp curvature are used. But for engines weighing 50 tons or more it would be better to have no turnout curve sharper than 10 or 12 degrees, if it were possible.

TURNOUTS FROM THE OUTSIDE OF CURVES.

By reference to diagrams Nos. 2 and 3, it is evident that the curvature of a turnout from the

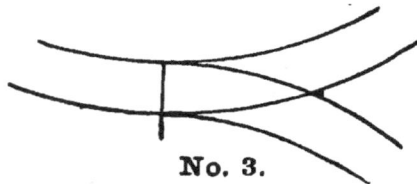

No. 3.

outside of a curve is less than that from the inside of a curve or from a straight track.

To find the degree of the turnout curve when it is from the outside, take the difference between the degree of the main-track curve and the degree of the curve of the frog, as given in Table No. 6.

Suppose the curvature of the main track is 4 degrees and the frog is a No. 8, the curvature suitable to which is $9\frac{1}{2}$ degrees, the difference between $9\frac{1}{2}$ degrees and 4 degrees is $5\frac{1}{2}$ degrees, which, in this case, is the degree of a turnout curve turning to the outside of the 4-degree curve.

If the curvature of the main track is about 10 degrees, the curvature of the turnout would be very light, practically a straight line, the difference being only about a half degree.

A No. 6 frog from the outside of an 8-degree curve will have about the same degree of curvature as a No. 8 frog from a straight track; that is, 17 degrees less 8 degrees, equal to 9 degrees.

This is worth remembering when putting in a turnout at the heel of a No. 8 frog to turn to the outside. If a No. 8 frog is used in such a case, the curvature through it will be less than that of the frog ahead; whereas, if a No. 6 is used its curve will be about the same as that of the No. 8, and it will make a much better turnout.

If, however, it is intended to connect with a parallel track, then use a No. 8, or the same number as the other frog, and put it in line with the other frog, just as in the case of a ladder track.

The following tables give the degree of the turnout curve when the frog is upon either the inside or the outside of curves from 1 to 9 degrees.

TABLE No. 5.

WHEN FROG IS UPON THE INSIDE OF THE CURVE.

FROG No.	CURVE FROM STRAIGHT LINE.	1°	2°	3°	4°	5°	6°	7°	8°	9°
	Degrees.	Deg.	Deg.	Deg.	Deg.	Deg.	Deg.	Deg.	Deg.	Deg.
6	17	18	19	20	21	22	23	24	25	26
7	12½	13½	14½	15½	16½	17½	18½	19½	20½	21½
8	9½	10½	11½	12½	13½	14½	15½	16½	17½	18½
9	7½	8½	9½	10½	11½	12½	13½	14½	15½	16½
10	6	7	8	9	10	11	12	13	14	15
11	5	6	7	8	9	10	11	12	13	14
12	4	5	6	7	8	9	10	11	12	13
15	2½	3½	4½	5½	6½	7½	8½	9½	10½	11½

TABLE No. 6.

WHEN FROG IS UPON THE OUTSIDE OF THE CURVE.

FROG No.	CURVE FROM STRAIGHT LINE.	1°	2°	3°	4°	5°	6°	7°	8°	9°
	Degrees.	Deg.	Deg.	Deg.	Deg.	Deg.	Deg.	Deg.	Deg.	Deg.
4	38½	37½	36½	35½	34½	33½	32½	31½	30½	29½
5	24½	23½	22½	21½	20½	19½	18½	17½	16½	15½
6	17	16	15	14	13	12	11	10	9	8
7	12½	11½	10½	9½	8½	7½	6½	5½	4½	3½
8	9½	8½	7½	6½	5½	4½	3½	2½	1½	
9	7½	6½	5½	4½	3½	2½	1½			
10	6	5	4	3	2	1				

In the first column are the frog numbers; in the next is the degree of curvature for each frog when the turnout is from a straight line; in the other columns is given for each frog the degree of curvature when the turnout is from any curve from 1 to 9 degrees.

To use these tables, suppose it should be

necessary to put in a turnout from the inside of a 6-degree curve and, at the same time, it should be desirable that the curvature of the turnout should not exceed 12 degrees, what frog should be used? Look in Table No. 5, and in the eighth column, under 6 degrees, 12 is found; opposite 12, in the first column, is 10; 10, then, is the number of the frog to be used. For any desired curvature for any other frog proceed in the same manner.

Suppose again, that it is desired to know the curvature of a No. 8 frog upon the inside of a 7-degree curve. Look in the first column, Table No. 5, for No. 8 frog, and opposite it, in the ninth column, under 7 degrees, find 16½ degrees, which is the degree of the desired curve. Any other degree is found in the same manner.

Again, this question may arise: Is it advisable to have a No. 6 turnout upon the inside of a 3-degree curve? The answer is, No; because by reference to Table No. 5 the curvature will be found to be about 20 degrees, which is too sharp for ordinary service.

Referring to Table No. 6, suppose a turnout is to be upon the outside of a 6-degree curve, what frog will give a turnout curve not to exceed the curvature of main track? A No. 7 frog will do it. Look in the eighth column, Table No. 6,

and under 6 degrees, 6½ degrees is found opposite No. 7 in the first column.   No. 7, therefore,
is the frog which should be used, 6½ degrees being the nearest degree of curvature.

Suppose again, that it is desired to know the
curvature of a No. 8 frog upon the outside of a
4-degree curve.   Find No. 8 frog in first column,
Table No. 6, and opposite it, under 4 degrees,
in sixth column, is 5½ degrees; 5½ degrees is,
therefore, the curvature desired.

When a turnout is upon the outside of a
curve it is preferable to use a frog which will
give a turnout curve somewhat similar in degree
to that of the main curve, instead of using one
which will make the turnout curve flat as com-
pared to the main curve.   Frogs of high numbers, that is, those above a No. 8 or 10, should,
therefore, not be used ordinarily in such cases.

In ordinary practice there are not many cases,
whether upon the inside or outside of a curve,
which cannot be fully met by using a No. 6, 8,
or 10 frog, so that it is rarely necessary to use
higher than these numbers, unless high speed is
attained or the main-track curve is very sharp.

THE STUB LEAD.

The stub lead, like the point lead, is measured along the straight rail—A to B.

There is no simple rule for obtaining the stub lead for all frogs and gauges, as is the case with the point lead. This is on account of there being so many different throws for the switch rails.

The "throw" of a stub switch is the distance the slide or moving rail moves at the head-block

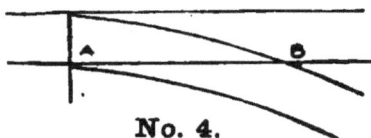

No. 4.

A, and every throw requires a different lead. The throws for standard gauges are 5, 5½, or 5¾ inches—5 inches predominating.

The lead for a stub switch for 4 feet 8½ inch and 4 feet 9 inch gauges is, approximately, 6¾ times the frog number for 5-inch throw, and 6½ times the frog number for 5¾-inch throw.

In the following table are leads which, although approximate, are nearly correct. In Table No. 9 are given the correct leads.

(29)

TABLE No. 7.

APPROXIMATE STUB LEADS, 4 FEET 8½ INCH AND
4 FEET 9 INCH GAUGES.

5-INCH THROW.			5¾-INCH THROW.		
Frog No.	Times.	Lead.	Frog No.	Times.	Lead.
		Feet. Inches.			Feet. Inches.
6	6¾	40 6	6	6½	39 0
7	6¾	47 3	7	6½	45 6
8	6¾	54 0	8	6½	52 0
9	6¾	60 9	9	6½	58 6
10	6¾	67 6	10	6½	65 0
11	6¾	74 3	11	6½	71 6
12	6¾	81 0	12	6½	78 0

The stub lead should not be shortened; it
and the theoretical length of switch rail should
be equal, or nearly so, to the full theoretical
lead.

A formula by which the stub lead can be cal.
culated for any gauge, throw, and frog, is:—

Stub lead, or $l = 2n \left(g - \sqrt{gt} \right)$, in which

l equals stub lead,

n equals frog number,

g equals gauge,

t equals throw.

This means that the stub lead is equal to the
gauge, minus the square root of the product of
the gauge and throw, multiplied by twice the
number of the frog.

To make this formula easily used, in the following table it is partially worked out for the gauges and throws most generally used, it only remaining to multiply the distances in the table following by twice the frog number to obtain the stub lead for any frog.

TABLE No. 8.

3 FEET GAUGE.			4 FEET 8½ INCH GAUGE.			4 FT. 9 IN. GAUGE.	
Throw.	$(g-\sqrt{gt})$		Throw.	$(g-\sqrt{gt})$		$(g-\sqrt{gt})$	
Inches.	Feet.	Inches.	Inches.	Feet.	Inches.	Feet.	Inches.
3	2	8¾	5	3	3¾	3	4
3½	2	8½	5½	3	3	3	3¼
4	2	8¼	5¾	3	2½	3	3

For any stub lead multiply the distance opposite the throw by twice the frog number.

What is the stub lead of No. 9 frog, 4 feet 8½ inch gauge and 5-inch throw? Multiply 3 feet 3¾ inches, opposite 5-inch throw, by twice the frog number, or 18, and we have 59 feet 7 inches as the stub lead.

Give stub lead of No. 8 frog, 4 feet 9 inch gauge and 5¾-inch throw. 3 feet 3 inches, opposite 5¾-inch throw, multiplied by 16, or twice No. 8 frog, is equal to 52 feet, or the stub lead desired.

The stub lead need not be exact. The same liberty in departing from it, however, cannot be taken as with the theoretical point lead, and, so far as it can be done, the calculated stub lead should be adhered to; not, however, to the extent of wasting rail by cutting so as to get the exact lead.

Do not use a stub lead for frogs higher than 10 or 12, as the curvature of the switch rail will be greater than the curvature from the headblock to the frog point.

The leads given in Table No. 7 are only approximately correct. If the correct lead is desired it can be found in the table below.

TABLE No. 9.

CORRECT STUB LEADS FOR DIFFERENT THROWS.

FROG No.	4 FEET 8½ INCHES.						4 FEET 9 INCHES.						SWITCH RAIL.
	5 In.		5½ In.		5¾ In.		5 In.		5½ In.		5¾ In.		
	Ft.	In.	Ft.	In.	Ft.	In.	Ft.	In.	Ft.	In.	Ft.	In.	Feet.
4	26	6	25	11	25	8	26	9	26	2	26	0	12
5	33	1	32	5	32	1	33	5	32	9	32	6	15
6	39	9	38	11	38	6	40	2	39	4	39	0	18
7	46	4	45	5	44	11	46	10	45	10	45	6	21
8	52	11	51	10	51	4	53	6	52	5	52	0	24
9	59	7	58	4	57	9	60	2	59	0	58	6	26
10	66	2	64	10	64	2	66	11	65	6	65	0	26
11	72	9	71	4	70	7	73	7	72	0	71	6	26
12	79	5	77	9	77	0	80	3	78	7	78	0	26

SWITCH OR MOVING RAILS.

One of the things in regard to which track-men are generally ignorant is the correct length of the switch or moving rail of a stub switch.

It is not unusual to see it the same length for all frogs without regard to what the throw may be.

Practically it does not make much difference, except in frogs less than No. 8, but every fore-man ought to know what is the proper length and how to obtain it.

A good moving rail is made by cutting a few inches off a 30-foot rail.

It should always be spiked to not less than 3 cross-ties and not less than 4 feet from the end of the rail, no difference for what frog or throw it may be, nor what may be given as the correct theoretical length of the moving rail.

The spiking point nearest the head-block is, in theory, the beginning of the turnout curve, and to that point—that is, to the point of the turnout curve—so far as practicable, the rails should be spiked solid, but beyond it, held to gauge only by the switch-rods, they should be left to adjust themselves to conform to the turn-out curve.

For every different frog and throw the distance from the head-block to the last spiking point is different, and this variable distance is called the theoretical length of the moving rail. The theoretical moving rail for a No. 10 frog and 5¾-inch throw is 30 feet, but as rails are only 30 feet long this theoretical length must be reduced to about 26 feet, which is about the longest practicable length of moving rail.

The following is a table of practicable lengths of the moving rail.

TABLE No. 10.

FOR 4 FEET 8½ INCHES, 4 FEET 9 INCHES, 3 FEET GAUGES.

FROG No.	4 FEET 8½ AND 4 FEET 9 INCHES.		3 FEET.
	5 Inches.	5¾ Inches.	4 Inches.
	Feet. Inches.	Feet.	Feet.
4	11 0	12	8
5	13 9	15	10
6	16 6	18	12
7	19 3	21	14
8	22 0	24	16
9	24 9	26	18
10	26 0	26	20
11	26 0	26	22

This may be condensed into the following rule: For 4 feet 8½ and 4 feet 9 inch gauges and 5-inch throw, the length of the moving rail is 2¾ (or 2.75) times the frog number, and for 5¾-inch throw it is 3 times the frog number.

For 3 feet gauge and 4-inch throw it is twice the frog number.

A few inches less than 30 feet is a good length of rail to make a moving rail, for the reason that there are always on hand old 30-foot rails with battered ends which can be cut off.

There is no advantage in using in a stub switch a frog higher than No. 10 or 11, because, it being impossible to make the moving rails the required theoretical length for frogs above these numbers, the curvature of the moving rails would be sharper than the turnout curve from the head-block to the point of the frog, and what would be gained by a frog of high number or small angle with decreased curvature would be lost by the increased curvature of the moving rails.

THE FROG NUMBER.

The "number" of a frog means the same as what is called the "proportion" of a frog. A 1 to 7 frog is in the "proportion," properly the ratio, of 1 foot wide to 7 feet long, and is the same as a No. 7; or a 1 to 10 the same as a No. 10.

The number of a frog corresponds to its length from point to heel divided by its width at the heel measured from gauge to gauge of the rails forming the frog angle.

It is important that the trackman should be able to distinguish one number of frog from another, and he should bear in mind that all frogs of the same width at the heel may not be the same number. The width at the heel is greater or less according to the distance from the point to the heel; and the way to do in every case of uncertainty is to measure the frog as explained on pages 37, 38, and 39.

There is no uniform length of frog from point to heel; that distance is therefore liable to be as various as there are frog makers.

A 1 to 8 frog, or a No. 8, at 8 inches from the theoretical frog point in the direction of the heel is 1 inch wide, and at 8 feet it is 1 foot wide, or 1 wide to 8 long, whether it is inches or feet, and it is always measured from gauge to gauge.

A 1 to 10, or No. 10, at 10 inches from the point is 1 inch wide, and at 10 feet it is one foot wide, or 1 wide to 10 long.

One way to obtain the number of any frog is to first ascertain accurately where the theoretical point of the frog is, it being the intersection of the sides of the frog as shown and explained on page 43; then take a foot rule and find where the frog measures exactly 4 inches wide, from gauge to gauge, C to D, back of the point, as shown in the diagram :—

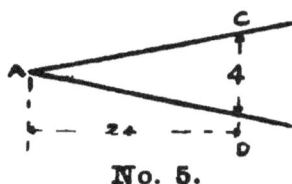

No. 5.

From where it is 4 inches wide measure the distance to the intersection of the gauge lines at the theoretical frog point A, and divide this distance in inches by 4 inches, the width, and as many times as it is greater than the 4 inches in width will be equal to the frog number.

Twenty-four inches divided by 4 inches is equal to 6, or a No. 6 frog.

Thirty-two inches divided by 4 inches is equal to 8, or a No. 8 frog.

The following is a table of the distance for different frogs from where the width is 4 inches to the theoretical point A.

TABLE No. 11.

MEASUREMENTS TO OBTAIN FROG NUMBER.

Frog No.	Distance.	Width.	Frog No.	Distance.	Width.
	Inches.	Inches.		Inches.	Inches.
4	16	4	9	36	4
5	20	4	10	40	4
6	24	4	11	44	4
7	28	4	12	48	4
8	32	4	15	60	4

The frog number can also be obtained in another way. Take a lead-pencil, or a stick about as long or a little longer than a pencil, and find where the width of the frog, gauge to gauge, is exactly equal to the length of the stick or pencil; from this point, by trial, find how many times greater than the stick or pencil the distance is to the theoretical point A.

If it is 6 times greater, the frog is a No. 6; if 8 times, it is a No. 8, and so on.

By a careful use of the pencil or stick the frog number can readily be ascertained.

Another way is to take the frog-boards re-ferred to on page 45, and place them one by one upon the frog until that one is found whose sides coincide with the gauge lines of the frog, and the board corresponding to the frog being numbered, the frog number is at once known.

Another way is to divide the total length of the frog from heel to toe by the sum of the width at the heel and at the toe. For example, if the total length is 15 feet, or 180 inches, and the width at the heel 8 inches and at the toe 7 inches, their sum would be 15 inches; dividing 180 by 15 the frog would be No. 12, as 12 times 15 are equal to 180.

In measuring at the toe the distance between the inside of the rails should be taken, whereas at the heel the distance to be used is between the outside of the rails, or the gauge lines in both cases.

THE FROG ANGLE.

It would not be necessary for the trackman to know anything about the frog angle, except to prevent his confusing it with the "propor-tion" of a frog and also the frog number.

What is called the "proportion" of a frog is the measure of the spread or divergence of the two sides of the frog in inches or feet; as, for

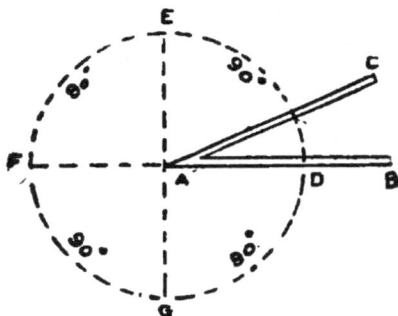

No. 6.

example, in a No. 8 frog, at every 8 inches from the point in the direction of the heel, the distance across is 1 inch, or at every 8 feet it is 1 foot, or in the "proportion" of 1 to 8. Correctly speaking, it is the ratio of 1 to 8.

The frog angle is also the spread or divergence of the two sides of the frog, but the expression for its measure is in terms of the degree and minute, which expressions are used only in con-

nection with the surveying instrument and cal-
culations, and, therefore, of no important use to
the foreman in his practical work.

In explanation of the word degree, as it re-
lates to a frog (see diagram No. 6), every circle,
however large or small, is divided into 360 equal
parts or spaces, each of which is called a "degree."

Beginning at D in the diagram, from D to E
it is 90 degrees, from D to F 180 degrees, from
D to G 270 degrees, and from D to D 360 degrees, completing the circle. So if the lines A
B C represent the angle of a frog, the point of
which is in the centre of the circle, the amount
of the divergence or angle of its two sides will
be as many degrees as are included between the
the sides A B and A C, the number of the
degrees being different for each frog number.

Below is a table of frog-angles corresponding
to frogs of different number.

TABLE No. 12.
FROG ANGLES.

Frog No.	Frog Angle.	Frog No.	Frog Angle.
4	14° 15	9	6° 22′
5	11 25	10	5 44
6	9 32	11	5 12
7	8 10	12	4 46
8	7 09	15	4 24

In explanation of the table, 14° 15′ means
14 degrees and 15 minutes, and 11° 25′ means
11 degrees and 25 minutes.

If the diagram represented a No. 6 frog, for
example, its spread or divergence would be
about 9½ of the 90 degrees from D to E.

The numbers in the column under "Frog
Angle" represent the degrees and minutes, the
latter being the expression of the measure of
anything less than a degree. The angle of No. 4
frog, for example, is 14 degrees and 15 minutes,
or 14¼ degrees, 15 being one-fourth of 60, the
number of minutes in a degree.

Any difference in the gauge of the track does
not affect the frog angle, the angle of a No. 8
frog in a 4 feet 9 inch gauge being the same
as for the same frog in a 3 feet gauge.

THE FROG POINT.

There is perhaps nothing in the detail of switch work which the trackman is so apt to regard as unimportant, or of which he knows so little and yet which is so important, as to properly understand what is the theoretical point of the frog and use it in his measurements.

What is usually understood by him as the point of the frog is the half-inch blunt point B, in the diagram below.

It is true it is a point of the frog, but it is the actual or practical point, and not the correct or

No. 7.

theoretical point, which should be used by him in his measurements.

The correct point is the intersection, A, of the gauge lines of the two sides of the frog forming the angle, and it is several inches beyond the half-inch blunt point, according to the number of the frog, and it is known as the theoretical point of frog.

(43)

To find where the theoretical point is, take two 2-foot rules or two straight-edges about 2 inches wide and 3 or 4 feet long, and place them along the gauge line of each side of the frog point, and where they meet, as A, is the theoretical point which should be used in all measurements to or from the frog point for leads or distance between frog points.

The practical point, B, should not be considered as being the point, as by doing so distances too great may be obtained, and, consequently, the frogs not being in their proper position, everything depending upon them will be likewise affected.

Too much stress cannot be laid upon the importance of this; as, for example, in a ladder track, if the first few frogs are a few inches out of their true position all the others will be out also; and in a cross-over, or where exact work may be necessary, even a few inches may make too much of a difference.

A FROG-BOARD.

For expeditious and accurate switch work a frog-board is indispensable.

It is simply a board sawed to correspond to the frog angle, and is used to locate frogs practically by moving or shifting it along the rail until the proper position of the frog is obtained, just as if the frog itself were used in the same manner.

It is usually made of dry pine, or any other light wood, about 1 inch thick, 6 to 12 inches wide, and 5 to 7 feet long, according to the length of the frog from point to heel.

The following diagram shows a frog-board :—

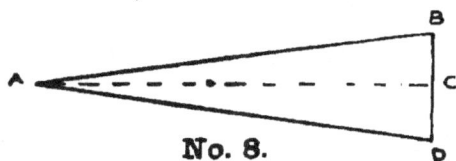

No. 8.

And in the following table are the dimen-sions necessary for marking out the board.

TABLE No. 13.

FROG-BOARD DIMENSIONS.

Frog No.	Length A to C.		Width B to D.	Frog No.	Length A to C.		Width B to D.
	Ft.	In.	Inches.		Ft.	In.	Inches.
4	4	0	12	9	6	0	8
5	5	0	12	10	5	0	6
6	5	0	10	11	5	6	6
7	5	3	9	12	6	0	6
8	6	0	9	15	6	3	5

To make, say a No. 8 board, draw a straight chalk or pencil line, A to C, through the middle of the board, and measure 6 feet (taken from table opposite No. 8 frog) from A to C; at C and at right angles to the line A C measure 4½ inches to B and D respectively, 4½ inches being one-half of 9 inches, the width B to D as in the table. Make a line from A to B and also from A to D, and saw out the board on those lines and it will be the correct angle.

For a No. 10 board the length from the point A to the end at C is 5 feet, and width 6 inches, or 3 inches on each side of the line, or a total of 6 inches, also taken from the table.

If a board longer than the length here given is desired, the lines forming the sides A to B and A to D can be extended as far as the total width of the board will permit, but in no case will it be necessary to have one longer than about 8 feet.

Mark upon each board clearly the frog number to which it corresponds. For this reason a surfaced board is to be preferred if it can be obtained.

The intelligent use of the frog-board, a ball of twine and a good tape-line will be found to be very helpful in all more than ordinary switch work, as by them all the frog points can be located beforehand, the string representing the gauge line of the frog rail, and no changing of frogs to improve the line will have to be done as the work is in progress; as not infrequently it happens that after the work is done it is evident that by a little change in the position of the frogs an improvement could have been made.

Frogs should never be located carelessly or their location guessed at. Use a board in every case of uncertainty or difficulty.

NUMBERS TO USE AND WHERE.

The proper selections of frogs suitable to the requirements of the various conditions of railroad service is important.

It may be necessary in sharp siding curves to use frogs less than a No. 6, but for ordinary conditions, if it can be avoided, it is not advisable to use even so low a number as No. 6.

The increased size and weight of engines is such that the turnout curve of a No. 8 frog, about $9\frac{1}{2}$ degrees, is as sharp a curve as ought to be used by the ordinary road engine.

Freight cars and engines made for sharp curvature can go around curves as high as 60 degrees easily, but as cases where this is necessary are rare, so far as possible, the limit should be about 10 degrees, or that corresponding to the curve of a No. 8 frog. It is, of course, frequently necessary to exceed this, but it should be avoided, if possible.

The kind of service to which the numbers most generally used are best adapted is as follows :—

No. 4 frog, for very sharp curves by very small engines.

No. 6 frog, for general use by small engines or occasional use by large engines.

No. 8 frog, for general use in heavy service by large engines.

No. 10 frog, for heavy service and usual speed to 20 miles an hour.

No. 12 frog, for usual speed 20 to 30 miles an hour.

No. 15 frog, for speed of 30 to 40, or more, miles an hour.

About the best numbers for ordinary service are Nos. 8, 9, and 10.

A No. 15 is suitable for turning out at high speed from one track to another. Anything higher in number than a 15 or 20 is neither necessary nor advisable.

There is no necessity of having so many frogs of different numbers. The even numbers, viz., 6, 8, 10, 12, and 16, are sufficient to meet all the requirements of any service, as are likewise the odd numbers 7, 9, 11, and 15. Either of these groups are recommended.

Half numbers are unnecessary, as all that is obtained by them can be obtained by using the nearest whole number, either by slightly changing the position of the frog or the alignment of the curve when it is placed in the track, without in the least impairing the efficiency of the turnout.

4

To the practice of adding turnout to turnout without any consideration of the future requirements or good alignment of the tracks for the purpose of avoiding a little extra work, may be attributed many objectionable combinations of frogs and annoying complications in switch work, and to avoid this it should be the endeavor to use nothing less than a No. 6 or a No. 8, and to arrange them so as in all cases to preserve symmetry and uniformity.

THE GAUGE AT THE FROG.

The proper gauging of frogs is more important than it is generally considered to be. In fact there is nothing in the detail of track work more important, so far as safety is concerned. The practice of leaving the gauge a little wide at the frog point should not be followed, except where the turnout curve is very sharp, or the turnout is upon a sharp main-track curve, the gauge of which then may have to be widened.

When it is necessary to widen the gauge at the frog, the guard-rail distance should always be increased exactly as much as the gauge is widened. If the guard-rail distance is 2 inches and if the gauge is widened $\frac{1}{2}$ inch, then the guard-rail distance should be $2\frac{1}{2}$ inches instead of 2 inches. It is a mistake to suppose that the all-important thing is to make the guard-rail distance exact, without regard to whether or not the gauge is exact.

The exact guard-rail distance is to be used only when the gauge is exact, as the important thing is the distance from the gauge line of the frog to that edge or side of the guard rail with which the passing wheel comes in contact, and which determines the distance the guard rail should be from the main rail. This distance is always equal to the gauge of the track less the guard-rail distance. For 4 feet 9 inch gauge and 2 inch guard-rail distance it is 4 feet 7 inches. For 4 feet $8\frac{1}{2}$ inch gauge and $1\frac{3}{4}$ inch guard-rail distance, it is 4 feet $6\frac{3}{4}$ inches.

WIDENING THE GAUGE OF CURVES.

It is not necessary to widen the gauge of all curves indiscriminately, simply because some curves above a certain degree may require it under certain conditions.

The difficulty generally is to keep track from becoming too wide, and it is important to know when and to what extent it is advisable to increase the gauge.

For example, the curvature of the legs of a "Y" is generally about 20 degrees, and it may be advisable to widen the gauge $\frac{1}{2}$ inch, or 4 feet 9 inches to 4 feet 9$\frac{1}{2}$ inches.

But if only 4 feet 8$\frac{1}{2}$ inch engines or cars use such a curve, then 4 feet 9 inches should not be exceeded, but if both 4 feet 8$\frac{1}{2}$ inch and 4 feet 9 inch engines or cars are to be provided for, then it is allowable to increase the 4 feet 8$\frac{1}{2}$ inch gauge to 4 feet 9$\frac{1}{2}$ inches.

In ordinary curvature, as high as about 10 degrees, the 4 feet 9 inch gauge requires no increase generally, but the 4 feet 8$\frac{1}{2}$ inch gauge may, on account of cars of wider gauge using it. It is necessary, therefore, in widening, to be governed by the necessity of providing for cars other than those to suit the gauge of the road.

The 4 feet 8½ inch gauge may, therefore, have to be widened something like in the following table :—

TABLE No. 14.

WIDENING THE GAUGE OF CURVES.

DEGREE OF CURVE.	For both 4 feet 8½ inch and 4 feet 9 inch wheels.	For either 4 feet 8½ inch or 4 feet 9 inch wheels only.
3	⅛ inch wide.	
4	¼ "	
6	¼ "	
8	⅜ "	
10	½ "	¼ inch wide.
12	⅝ "	¼ "
14	¾ "	⅜ "
16	⅞ "	⅜ "
18	1 "	½ "
20	1 "	½ "
30	1 "	¾ "

To enable a sharp curve to be used safely, in addition to widening the gauge, there should be little, if any, elevation. A 20-degree curve needs no elevation if the speed is slow.

When it is necessary to widen the gauge of a turnout curve the maximum or greatest increase should be at the frog point, and the increase from the gauge at the switch, where it is neat, to the frog, where it is widest, should be made gradually. When the gauge has been increased at the frog point the guard rail should be the same distance from the frog it would be if the gauge were exact, the guard-rail distance increasing as much as the gauge is widened. Divide the increase in the gauge by two or four, and make the gauge correspondingly wide at each one-fourth or one-half point of the lead.

Suppose the lead is 48 feet and the gauge has been widened $\frac{1}{2}$ inch. If the gauge is 4 feet 9 inches, 12 feet from the switch point it would be 4 feet $9\frac{1}{8}$ inches; at 24 feet it would be 4 feet $9\frac{1}{4}$ inches; at 36 feet, 4 feet $9\frac{3}{8}$ inches; and at 48 feet, or the frog point, it would be 4 feet $9\frac{1}{2}$ inches, or $\frac{1}{2}$ inch wide.

The same results can be obtained by first gauging the track accurately and then placing the guard rail the required distance from the main rail, and this is the way it is generally done; but when the gauge is widened or the guard-rail distance carelessly measured, the effect is seen upon the frog and guard rail. Every foreman should be provided with a guard-rail gauge, not combined with but separate from his track gauge, and no guard rail should be set without it.

On tangents or light curves there should be no variation whatever from the exact gauge or guard-rail distance.

A frog upon the high side of a curve may cause a noticeable lurch to the passing train when in exact gauge and having the guard-rail distance exact, if the remainder of the curve is wide as to gauge, either made so or has become so from its natural tendency to widen. In such a case it might be well to make the gauge at the frog the same as that of the curve, but the guard rail should always be the same distance from the frog whether the gauge is exact or wide.

When a frog is upon the low side of a curve the gauge should be kept as nearly exact as possible by rail braces upon the high side opposite the frog, and the changes in the gauge from being exact at the frog to what the curve may have become wide should be made gradually upon each side of the frog. In this case the wing rail of the frog acts as a guard rail upon the low side, and the wider the gauge the greater the blow and injury to the frog and liability to accident.

To gauge a frog properly the gauge should be placed at the heel and toe and the frog tacked at neat gauge, that is, held in position by the spikes about half driven; then bring the frog to neat gauge at a point from six to twelve inches back of the blunt point, where there is no bevel. The beveled point really makes the gauge a little wide where it may be needed to be so, so there is no necessity of increasing it upon straight line. All gauging should be done so that the gauge will fall into place easily and fit neatly.

The distance between the wing rail and the point or tongue of the frog, also at the point between the frog point and toe, where the two wing rails are closest, is usually the same as the guard-rail distance.

The two guard-rail distances most generally used are 2 inches for 4 feet 9 inch gauge and $1\frac{3}{4}$ inches for 4 feet $8\frac{1}{2}$ inch gauge.

Some of the evidences of improper gauging are :—

1. When the guard rail or the wing rail of the frog is unnaturally worn by the flange and difficult to be kept in position, making many rail braces necessary.

2. When near the end of the guard rail there is an abrupt change from a badly worn rail head to a full head through the guard rail upon the high side of the curve.

3. When there is a similar mark at either end of the frog when it is upon the high side of the curve.

4. When the frog receives a blow from the passing wheel or shows evidence of unnatural strain by pulling apart.

Whenever these evidences are found, the gauging should at once be gone over and corrected.

Additional guard-rail chairs or rail braces are not infrequently used to remedy the difficulties just mentioned, but the necessity for frogs and guard rails to be supported so fully is an evidence of ignorance as to the real cause of the trouble.

Guard rails cannot easily be kept to the exact guard-rail distance, but when they exceed by $\frac{1}{4}$ of an inch the required distance, they should be taken up and relaid. Whenever a reasonable number of guard-rail chairs are not sufficient to hold the frog or guard rail in position, there is something wrong with the gauging and it should be attended to promptly.

TO LINE TURNOUT CURVES.

It is the almost uniform practice to line the turnout curve, called "lining the lead," entirely by the eye; and although it can be done in that way very well, there is, however, a way by which the curvature of the turnout can be obtained more rapidly and accurately than is obtained by the eye alone. This method is that of locating by ordinates two or three points of the turnout curve, as shown in the diagram below.

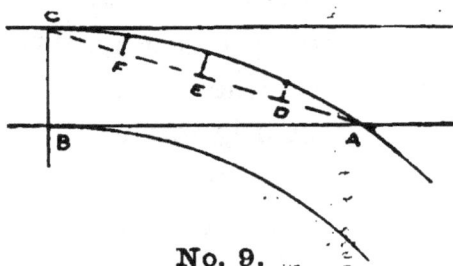

No. 9.

In this diagram, A is the theoretical point of frog, and C is the point or beginning of the theoretical curve, not always the point of the switch, as might be supposed. What is wanted by the trackman is the correct alignment or line of the curve from A to C, or from the frog point to the switch.

The straight line between A and C is called the chord, and the distances from it to the curve at D, E, and F are called ordinates. By measuring from the frog point A along the chord a certain distance to D, E, and F respectively, and from these points at right angles, by measuring certain other distances to the curve, all of which are given in the Tables Nos. 15, 16, and 17, three points of the turnout curve may be located, and having, in addition, the point of frog and point of switch already located, all that is necessary to be done is to line between these points to obtain the correct alignment of the curve.

When any lining of this kind is to be done, having decided upon the location of the frog, the first thing to do is to locate the point of the turnout curve C. This may be done by measuring the theoretical lead from A to B, C being directly opposite B, upon the other rail. Make a chalk-mark at C, the beginning of the curve, and stretch a string from A, the theoretical point of the frog, to C, the point of the curve, not the point of the switch, unless the frog has the full theoretical lead. The string corresponds to the line from A to C, and the offsets from this line to the curve are the ordinates.

The ordinates at D and F are called quarter ordinates because they are each at a point one-fourth the distance from the point of the frog to the point of the theoretical curve at C.

The ordinate at E is called the "middle ordinate" because it is midway between the point of the frog and the point of the curve at C.

The middle ordinate is equal to one-fourth the gauge for No. 5 frogs and over, and when the gauge does not vary far from 4 feet 9 inches.

For 4 feet $8\frac{1}{2}$ inch gauge it is, therefore, 1 foot $2\frac{1}{8}$ inches, and for 4 feet 9 inches it is 1 foot $2\frac{1}{4}$ inches.

The quarter ordinates are $\frac{3}{16}$ the gauge, or $10\frac{5}{8}$ inches for 4 feet $8\frac{1}{2}$ inch and $10\frac{3}{4}$ inches for 4 feet 9 inch gauges.

The full theoretical lead, as given in the tables, should always be used to find, by measurement, the point of curve at C, even if the lead is shortened.

The following tables give the distance or lead to be measured from the frog point to find the point of curve. They give also the middle and quarter ordinates at the proper distance from the frog point for different frogs and gauges :—

TABLE No. 15.

FOR 4 FEET 8½ INCH GAUGE.

FROG No.	THEORETICAL LEAD.		FROG POINT TO ORDINATES.				DIAGONAL DISTANCE, A TO C.	
			Quarter, 10⅝ Inches.		Middle, 1 Ft. 2⅛ In.			
	Ft.	In.	Feet.	Inches.	Feet.	Inches.	Feet.	Inches.
4	37	8	9	6	19	0	38	0
5	47	1	11	10	23	8	47	4
6	56	6	14	5	28	10	56	8
7	65	11	16	6	33	0	66	1
8	75	4	18	11	37	9	75	6
9	84	9	21	3	42	5	84	11
10	94	2	23	7	47	2	94	4
11	103	7	25	11	51	10	103	8
12	113	0	28	3	56	7	113	1
15	141	3	35	4	70	8	141	4

Note that 1 foot 2⅛ inches is the middle ordinate and 10⅝ inches is for both quarter ordinates. Measurement always to be taken from the theoretical point of the frog, along the string to the point where the ordinate is measured.

TABLE No. 16.

FOR 4 FEET 9 INCH GAUGE.

FROG No.	THEORETI- CAL LEAD.		FROG POINT TO ORDINATES.				DIAGONAL DISTANCE, A TO C.	
			Quar'er, 10¾ Inches.		Middle, 1 Ft. 2¼ In.			
	Ft.	In.	Feet.	Inches.	Feet.	Inches.	Feet.	Inches.
4	38	0	9	7	19	2	38	4
5	47	6	11	11	23	10	47	9
6	57	0	14	4	28	7	57	2
7	66	6	16	8	33	4	66	8
8	76	0	19	0	38	1	76	2
9	85	7	21	5	42	10	85	9
10	95	0	23	9	47	7	95	1
11	104	6	26	2	52	4	104	7
12	114	0	28	6	57	0	114	1
15	142	6	35	8	71	4	142	7

Note that 1 foot 2¼ inches is the middle ordinate and 10¾ inches is for both quarter ordinates. Measurement to be taken from the theoretical point of the frog, along the string to the point where the ordinate is measured.

TABLE No. 17.

FOR 3 FEET GAUGE.

FROG No.	THEORETI-CAL LEAD.		FROG POINT TO ORDINATES.				DIAGONAL DISTANCE, A TO C.	
			Quarter, 6¾ In.		Middle, 9 In.			
	Feet.	Inches.	Feet.	Inches.	Feet.	Inches.	Feet.	Inches
4	24	0	6	0	12	1	24	2
5	30	0	7	6	15	1	30	2
6	36	0	9	0	18	1	36	2
7	42	0	10	6	21	1	42	1
8	48	0	12	0	24	1	48	1
9	54	0	13	6	27	0	54	1
10	60	0	15	0	30	0	60	1

Note that 9 inches is the middle ordinate and 6¾ inches is for both quarter ordinates. Measurement always to be taken from the theoretical point of the frog.

To explain the use of these tables, suppose it is desired to line the turnout curve of a No. 8 frog, 4 feet 9 inch gauge. Refer to Table No. 16, and in column giving theoretical lead of a No. 8 frog, 76 feet is found. Measure the lead A to B, 76 feet from the point of frog in the direction of the switch, and on the gauge of the rail at C, exactly opposite B, make a chalk-mark. The diagonal distance A to C, taken from the last column, may be measured to C, if there is at hand a tape-line long enough.

Stretch a line from point of frog to the chalk-mark at C, which is the point of the curve. This string is the line from which the ordinates are to be measured.

Refer again to table No. 16, and in the third column, opposite No. 8 frog, 19 feet is found to be the distance from the frog point to where the first quarter ordinate is measured. Measure along the line 19 feet from the frog point, and at this point bring the gauge of the rail of the turnout curve to $10\frac{3}{4}$ inches from the string and tack it with spikes.

Refer again to the table, and find that the middle ordinate is at 38 feet 1 inch from the frog point. Continue the measurement 38 feet 1 inch from the frog point, and bring the gauge of the rail to 1 foot $2\frac{1}{4}$ inches from the string and tack it. Two points of the curve, one at the middle and the other at the quarter ordinate, are thus established.

With the point of switch, point of frog, and these two points all located, all that is necessary to be done to finish is to line between all the points with the eye, and the correct curvature is obtained.

If the distance from the frog places the second quarter ordinate, at F, upon a split switch or slide rail of a stub switch, this ordinate may be

5

omitted, as the heel of the split switch or the head-block of the stub switch locates its position with reference to the turnout curve.

The diagonal distance in the last column of the tables is the distance in a straight line from the point of frog to the point, C, of the theoretical curve. By using it and measuring with a 100-foot tape-line the point of the curve can be found, perhaps, more easily than by measuring the lead, but having only a 50-foot tape-line the easiest way is to measure the lead and move over to the opposite rail, as directed.

THE LINE AT THE HEEL OF THE FROG.

In lining the curve at the heel of the frog in a turnout when it reverses into a parallel track, a very common mistake is made in beginning the curve at the frog point. The supposition is, and it is true, that the curvature at the heel of the frog should be the same as that between the frog and the switch, and yet in lining, notwithstanding the greatest care may be exercised, a good curve cannot be obtained. The reason is this: A single turnout is equivalent to a crossover between two parallel tracks. In the latter there should be straight line between the frog points. There should, likewise, be straight line from the point of the frog in a turnout for the distance the same frogs would be apart in a cross-over.

The distance the line should be straight is given in the following table for 4 feet $8\frac{1}{2}$ inch and 4 feet 9 inch gauges :—

TABLE No. 18.

LENGTH OF TANGENT AT HEEL OF FROG.

FROG No.	DISTANCE BETWEEN TRACKS.					
	6 Feet 6 Inches.		7 Feet.		7 Feet 6 Inches.	
	Feet.	Inches.	Feet.	Inches.	Feet.	Inches.
6	10	6	13	6	16	6
7	12	3	15	9	19	3
8	14	0	18	0	22	0
9	15	9	20	3	24	9
10	17	6	22	6	27	6
11	19	3	24	9	30	3
12	21	0	27	0	33	0
15	26	3	33	9	41	3

At a point about 50 feet back of the frog, first measure the distance between the tracks which are connected by the turnout, and refer to the table above, and in the column under the distance nearest that obtained by measurement, and opposite the number of the frog that is in the turnout, is found the length of the straight line. If, for example, the frog is No. 8 and the distance between tracks 7 feet 6 inches, the straight line or tangent is 22 feet. Make it straight for 22 feet and from there curve for a distance equal to the lead of about 9½ times the frog number, which, in this case, would be 76 feet. This curve will be the same, practically, as that at the toe of the frog and its length equal to that of the theoretical lead,

It is not necessary to have the exact distance between the tracks. Those in the table are near enough. Nor is it necessary to have more than a reasonable length of straight line at the heel of the frog, keeping somewhat near the distances in the table.

CROSS-OVERS UPON STRAIGHT LINE.

A through crossing or cross-over is made up of two single turnouts facing in opposite directions and connected between the frogs by a piece of straight track. What is true of the turnout in regard to the lead, &c., is true also of those forming the cross-over, the only thing in anywise difficult being to connect them, that is, to find the position of the second frog. This can be done in various ways, theoretically or practically, with equally satisfactory results generally.

In ordinary cross-overs between straight and parallel tracks the line between the frog points should always be straight, unless the distance between the tracks is so great that it is advisable to save distance by reversing at a point midway between the frog points.

But for the usual distance of seven or eight feet which tracks are apart in general railroad operation, there should always be straight line between the frogs.

The distance between tracks should not be

less than will permit a man to walk erect and comfortably between cars standing upon them. Seven feet between the outside of the rails, or about 7 feet 6 inches between the gauge lines, is sufficient to do this, and, so far as possible, anything less should be avoided .in laying new tracks or renewing old ones.

Parallel tracks should also be a uniform distance apart, whatever distance may be considered to be best; and work upon tracks not so should be done with a view to their all being thrown eventually to a uniform and sufficient distance apart.

Trackmen are accustomed to consider the distance between tracks as being between the outside of the rail heads, and to measure between them for the distance apart. This should not be done. The distance between the gauge lines, that is, between the inside or gauge side of the rails, should always be taken as the distance between tracks, for the reason that the gauge line or inside, not the outside, of rail head, is the basis of measurement in all switch and track work, or should be.

The foreman who has set frogs by measurement, and has not been satisfied with them, might have found that his lack of success was largely due to his not having taken the distance between gauge lines, it being a very common error not to do so.

The work of putting in a cross-over should be proceeded with in the same manner as that of putting in a single turnout. The location of either the frog point or head-block should first be decided upon, and no work should be done until the location of both head-blocks and both frog points have been made and clearly marked upon the rails, either accurately or approximately.

In deciding upon the location of the point of the first frog, so far as possible it should be the endeavor to place the heel or toe of the frog at a joint to avoid making a cut, unless the joints at the head-block, particularly in the case of a point or split switch, are so disposed as to make it better to first locate the point of the switch, in which event the location of the frog point will have to be determined by measurement, regardless of the joints. Having located either the point of the switch or the frog point, the other may be found as directed on pages 8–12.

When the location of the first frog has been made, and it is not particular which of the two is made first, the point of the second, or the one in the other parallel track, will be a distance from the point of the first frog, measured along the straight or parallel track, varying according

to the frog number and the distance the tracks
are apart. What this distance between the frog
points is may be found approximately in every
case by the following rule :—

From the distance between gauge lines of the
parallel tracks subtract the gauge of the track
and multiply the remainder by the number of
the frog, and it will give the distance between
the frog points measured along the parallel tracks,
as C to B in the diagram.

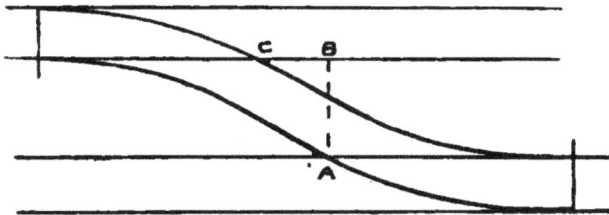

No. 10.

Suppose the distance between the gauge lines
is 7 feet 5 inches, the gauge 4 feet 9 inches, and
the frog a No. 8. The difference between 7 feet
5 inches and 4 feet 9 inches is 2 feet 8 inches.
Multiplying 2 feet 8 inches, or 32 inches, by 8,
we have 256 inches, equal to 21 feet 4 inches.
Measure this distance along the rail opposite the
frog, from C to B, in Diagram No. 10, which is
exactly opposite the point of the frog A. Place
the point of the second frog at A. Suppose the
distance between tracks is 7 feet, gauge 4 feet

8½ inches, and frog a No. 9. The distance from C to B would then be 20 feet 7 inches, obtained by the same process.

In the following tables are given the distances obtained by the rule just given, for 4 feet 8½ inch and 4 feet 9 inch gauges, for every 3 inches variation in the distance between gauge lines from 6 feet 6 inches to 8 feet. For any other distances the tracks are apart, the distance C to B can be obtained by the same rule.

TABLE No. 19.

DISTANCE BETWEEN FROG POINTS, MEASURED ALONG THE PARALLEL TRACK.

Gauge, 4 feet 8½ inches.

FROG No.	DISTANCE BETWEEN GAUGE LINES.							
	6 ft. 6 in.	6 ft. 9 in.	7 ft. o in.	7 ft. 3 in.	7 ft. 5 in	7 ft. 6 in.	7 ft. 9 in.	8 ft. o in.
	Ft. In.	Ft. In.	Ft. In.	Ft. In.	Ft. In.	Ft. In.	Ft. In.	Ft. In,
6	10 9	12 3	13 9	15 3	16 3	16 9	18 3	19 9
7	12 6	14 3	16 0	17 9	19 0	19 6	21 3	23 0
8	14 4	16 4	18 4	20 4	21 8	22 4	24 4	26 4
9	16 1	18 4	20 7	22 10	24 5	25 1	27 4	29 7
10	17 11	20 5	22 11	25 5	27 1	27 11	30 5	32 11
11	19 8	22 5	25 2	27 11	29 10	30 8	33 5	36 2
12	21 6	24 6	27 6	30 6	32 6	33 6	36 6	39 6
15	26 10	30 7	34 4	38 1	40 8	41 10	45 7	49 4

TABLE No. 20.

Gauge, 4 feet 9 inches.

FROG No.	DISTANCE BETWEEN GAUGE LINES.							
	6 ft. 6 in.	6 ft. 9 in.	7 ft. 0 in.	7 ft. 3 in.	7 ft. 5 in.	7 ft. 6 in.	7 ft. 9 in.	8 ft. 0 in.
	Ft. In.	Ft. In.	Ft. In.	Ft. In.	Ft. In.	Ft. In.	Ft. In.	Ft. In.
6	10 6	12 0	13 6	15 0	16 0	16 6	18 0	19 6
7	12 3	14 0	15 9	17 6	18 8	19 3	21 0	22 9
8	14 0	16 0	18 0	20 0	21 4	22 0	24 0	26 0
9	15 9	18 0	20 3	22 6	24 0	24 9	27 0	29 3
10	17 6	20 0	22 6	25 0	26 8	27 6	30 0	32 6
11	19 3	22 0	24 9	27 6	29 4	30 3	33 0	35 9
12	21 0	24 0	27 0	30 0	32 0	33 0	36 0	39 0
15	26 3	30 0	33 9	37 6	40 0	41 3	45 0	48 9

The distances in these tables, obtained by the rule given on page 73, are not exactly correct, but they can be used with excellent results, from the fact that the difference of a few inches does not seriously affect the line through the frogs.

There is no such simple rule by which the exact distance between frog points, measured along the parallel track, can be obtained. In Tables Nos. 21 and 22, however, are given the correct distances between the frogs, which, upon comparison, will be found to differ but slightly from those in Tables Nos. 19 and 20. The choice of these tables is left to the foreman, the preference, however, being in favor of those giving the correct distances.

TABLE No. 21.

Giving Correct Distances Between Frog Points, Measured Along Parallel Track.

Gauge, 4 feet 8½ inches.

Frog No.	Distance Between Gauge Lines.							
	6 ft. 6 in.	6 ft. 9 in.	7 ft. 0 in.	7 ft. 3 in.	7 ft. 5 in.	7 ft. 6 in.	7 ft. 9 in.	8 ft. 0 in.
	Ft. In.	Ft. In.	Ft. In.	Ft. In.	Ft. In.	Ft. In.	Ft. In.	Ft. In.
6	10 3	11 9	13 3	14 9	15 9	16 3	17 9	19 3
7	12 2	13 11	15 8	17 4	18 6	19 1	20 10	22 7
8	14 0	16 0	18 0	20 0	21 4	22 0	23 11	25 11
9	15 10	18 1	20 4	22 7	24 0	24 9	27 0	29 3
10	17 8	20 2	22 8	25 1	26 9	27 7	30 1	32 7
11	19 6	22 2	24 11	27 8	29 6	30 5	32 2	35 11
12	21 3	24 3	27 3	30 3	32 3	33 3	36 3	39 3
15	26 8	30 5	34 2	37 11	40 5	41 8	45 5	49 2

TABLE No. 22.

Gauge, 4 feet 9 inches.

Frog No.	Distance Between Gauge Lines.							
	6 ft. 6 in.	6 ft. 9 in.	7 ft. 0 in.	7 ft. 3 in.	7 ft. 5 in.	7 ft. 6 in.	7 ft. 9 in.	8 ft. 0 in.
	Ft. In.	Ft. In.	Ft. In.	Ft. In.	Ft. In.	Ft. In.	Ft. In.	Ft. In.
6	10 0	11 6	13 0	14 6	15 6	16 0	17 6	19 0
7	11 10	13 7	15 4	17 1	18 3	18 10	20 6	22 4
8	13 8	15 8	17 8	19 8	21 0	21 8	23 7	25 7
9	15 5	17 8	19 11	22 2	23 8	24 5	26 8	28 11
10	17 3	19 9	22 3	24 8	26 4	27 2	29 8	32 2
11	19 0	21 9	24 6	27 3	29 1	30 0	32 9	35 6
12	20 9	23 9	26 9	29 9	31 9	32 9	35 9	38 9
15	26 0	29 10	33 6	37 4	39 10	41 0	44 9	48 6

To use all these tables, first measure very carefully the distance between the gauge lines of the
tracks in which the cross-over is to be placed,
which, for example, will be supposed to be 7
feet 5 inches, the frogs being No. 8 and the
gauge 4 feet 9 inches.   In Table No. 22, look in
the column under 7 feet 5 inches and opposite
No. 8, and find 21 feet 0 inch.   This is the correct distance between the frog points along the
straight rail C to B, page 73.   The distance obtained by the rule, and found in Table No. 20,
is 21 feet 4 inches.

Should the distance between gauge lines be
one not given in the tables, for example, 6
feet 10 inches, and if the track cannot be thrown
to 6 feet 9 inches or 7 feet, then obtain the distance by the rule on page 73, in the manner already explained; or take the difference between
the distance for 7 feet and that for 6 feet 9
inches and divide it by 3, and add one-third or
two-thirds of the difference to 6 feet 9 inches, ac- ·
cording as the increase in the distance apart is 1
or 2 inches.

Another and easy way to ascertain the location
of the point of the second frog is to know what
the distance is in a straight line between the frog
points.   This distance we will call the diagonal
distance, and is from A to B in Diagram No. 11.

Suppose a crossing is to be put in between two straight and parallel tracks, as shown in the diagram, and that the location of the point of the first frog, at A, has been decided upon. If the diagonal distance between the frog points for any frog is given for certain distances between tracks, then a simple measurement of this distance from the point of one frog will determine where the point of the other should be.

From Table No. 24 we find that for 7 feet 5 inches between gauge lines, No. 8 frogs and 4

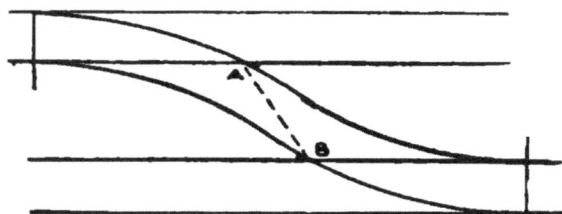

No. 11.

feet 9 inch gauge, the distance between frog points is 22 feet 3 inches. From the theoretical point of frog, if it is already in the track, or from a chalk-mark upon the gauge line of the rail where it is to be, if it is not, measure 22 feet 3 inches in a direction from A to B, and where this distance meets or intersects the gauge line of the opposite rail will be the point of the other frog. Mark it with chalk or a rail-cutter, and place the frog there.

The location of the point of the frog found in this manner should be the same as that obtained by measurement of the distance in Table No. 22, and if done accurately will be correct.

The following tables give the diagonal distance between the frog points :—

TABLE No. 23.

DIAGONAL DISTANCE BETWEEN FROG POINTS.

Gauge, 4 feet 8½ inches.

FROG NO.	DISTANCE BETWEEN GAUGE LINES OF TRACKS.							
	6 ft. 6 in.	6 ft. 9 in.	7 ft. 0 in.	7 ft. 3 in.	7 ft. 5 in.	7 ft. 6 in.	7 ft. 9 in.	8 ft. 0 in.
	Ft. In.	Ft. In.	Ft. In.	Ft. In.	Ft. In.	Ft. In.	Ft. In.	Ft. In.
6	12 1	13 7	15 0	16 5	17 5	17 11	19 4	20 10
7	13 9	15 5	17 2	18 10	20 0	20 6	22 3	24 0
8	15 5	17 4	19 3	21 3	22 6	23 3	25 2	27 2
9	17 1	19 3	21 6	23 9	25 1	25 11	28 1	30 4
10	18 9	21 3	23 9	26 1	27 9	28 7	31 1	33 7
11	20 6	23 2	25 10	28 7	30 5	31 4	33 1	35 10
12	22 3	25 2	28 2	31 1	33 1	34 1	37 1	40 1
15	27 6	31 2	34 11	38 7	41 1	42 4	46 1	49 10

TABLE No. 24.

Gauge, 4 feet 9 inches..

Frog No.	Distance Between Gauge Lines of Tracks.							
	6 ft. 6 in.	6 ft. 9 in	7 ft. o in.	7 ft. 3 in.	7 ft. 5 in.	7 ft. 6 in.	7 ft. 9 in.	8 ft. o in.
	Ft. In.	Ft. In.	Ft. In.	Ft. In.	Ft. In.	Ft. In.	Ft. In.	Ft. In.
6	11 11	13 4	14 9	16 3	17 2	17 8	19 2	20 7
7	13 6	15 2	16 10	18 7	19 9	20 3	21 11	23 9
8	15 1	17 0	19 0	20 11	22 3	22 11	24 10	26 10
9	16 9	18 11	21 1	23 4	24 10	25 6	27 9	30 0
10	18 5	20 10	23 4	25 9	27 4	28 2	30 8	33 2
11	20 1	22 9	25 6	28 2	30 0	30 11	33 8	36 5
12	21 9	24 8	27 8	30 8	32 7	33 7	36 7	39 7
15	25 10	30 7	34 3	38 0	40 6	41 8	45 5	49 2

To use these tables : Having first measured the distance between gauge lines of the two tracks, refer to the column under that distance, and opposite the frog number corresponding to that to be put in, will be found the diagonal distance between the frog points. Measure this carefully, as directed, and the frog point will be accurately located. Suppose in a 4 feet 8½ inch gauge and No. 9 frogs, the distance between gauge lines or tracks is 7 feet, what is the diagonal distance ?

By reference to Table No. 23, under 7 feet and opposite No. 9 frog, 21 feet 6 inches is found to be the distance desired. In the same manner find the diagonal distance for any other frogs.

If the distance between gauge lines is one not given in the tables, then find the frog point by the rule on page 73, or take the difference between the two distances nearest that which the tracks are apart and divide this difference by 3, and add one-third or two-thirds of it to the less distance, according as the increase is 1 or 2 inches.

Example: What is the diagonal distance, No. 8 frogs, 4 feet 9 inch gauge, and 6 feet 11 inches between gauge lines?

In Table No. 24, 17 feet is the distance for 6 feet 9 inches apart, and 19 feet for 7 feet apart; the difference is 2 feet, or 24 inches. Twenty-four divided by 3, equals 8 inches, which is equal to one-third of 24; two-thirds of 24 are twice 8, or 16 inches, equal to 1 foot 4 inches, which, added to 17 feet, makes 18 feet 4 inches, or the diagonal distance for 6 feet 11 inches between tracks.

Any objection to setting frogs by measurement, upon the ground that they are not made of the correct angle, and, therefore, cannot be set accurately in that way, is hardly warranted by the facts, as generally it is not only the easiest way but the best one, and frogs are made sufficiently accurate to enable it to be done generally.

6

Although it is well to bear in mind that the theoretical frog point is the one from or to which measurement should be made, there is no objection to measuring from the blunt point or any other well-defined mark at the frog point, provided the measurement is made to or from a corresponding point of the other frog.

Be careful to set the second frog of a cross-over upon a long tangent exactly right, as the good alignment of a long tangent is easily destroyed by a mistake of a few inches in locating the second frog.

To set frogs in a cross-over practically, a good way is to set the first frog and lay a full rail at its heel, connecting it with splices to the frog; then give this rail for its entire length the exact line or angle of the frog and tack it with spikes to hold it in line.   Place the track-gauge perpendicular to this rail and move it along the rail to the point where it meets the gauge line of the other rail.

This point will be the location of the point of the other or second frog.

Another way is : Having, as before, connected and lined a rail at the heel of the frog already in track, take a frog-board corresponding to the frog number and place it upon the frog rail of the opposite track, keeping its side exactly parallel with the gauge line, and, with the track-gauge perpendicular to the rail, as before, move the board along the rail to the point where the gauge is exact at both the point and the heel of the frog-board, and the frog will be accurately located, the point of the board being the same as the point of the frog.

CROSS-OVERS UPON CURVES.

On account of the wide difference in the curvature of main-track curves it is impossible to give a simple, practical rule for the distance between the frogs in a cross-over upon a curve. When one is to be put in, about as good a method as any is to set the frog practically by the frog-board, as explained on page 82, in

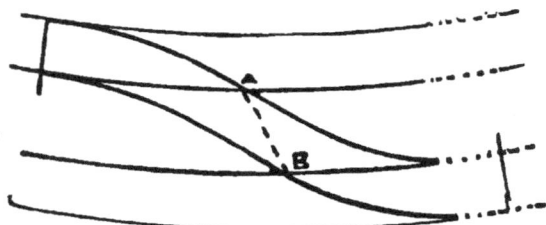

No. 12.

which case the alignment between the frog points may be straight or curved, according to the circumstances or the desire. If the curve is sharp and a No. 8 frog or less is used, the curvature of the lead of the frog upon the inside of the curve will be very sharp, as referred to at length on page 22. This, however, could be reduced by making a curve between the frog points which would enable a frog of higher number than otherwise to be placed upon the inside of the curve, and consequently a longer lead and less curvature could be obtained for it.

The amount of curvature of the turnout and also that desired between the frog points will depend upon the number or angle of the frogs available for the inside of the curve.

As will be seen by Table No. 25, the number of the frog upon the inside of a curve, except in frogs less than No. 8, is always less than that upon the outside when there is straight line between them; and also the frog number decreases as the curvature and distance between tracks increase.

It is customary to place in a cross-over upon a curve two frogs of the same number, just as is done upon a straight line; but frogs only as high as No. 7 will give straight line between them when the tracks are 6 to 8 feet apart and the curvature is as high as 8 or 10 degrees.

Two No. 8 frogs will also give straight line upon curves as high as 3 degrees for the same distances apart, but upon curves from 3 to 10 degrees they will give straight line only when distance the tracks are apart is less than 7 feet 3 inches.

Whenever two frogs of the same number higher than No. 8 are used, it is necessary to make a curve between them and to find the location of the point of the second frog practically. But, ordinarily, straight line between the frogs is sufficient, and it can be obtained if the proper combination of frogs is used.

Table No. 25 gives the combinations of the frogs for cross-overs upon curves, and also the diagonal distance between the frog points A to B, as shown in Diagram 12, for every 3 inches difference in distance between gauge lines of track from 6 feet 6 inches to 8 feet, when the line between the frogs is straight, the first frog located being upon the outside of the curve.

In explanation: Suppose we want to know the number of the second frog upon the inside of a curve, and also where its point will be if a No. 10 is placed upon the outside of a 6-degree curve and the distance between the gauge lines of the parallel tracks is 7 feet 5 inches. Refer to Table No. 25, under 7 feet 5 inches, opposite No. 10, the outside frog, we find the inside frog is a No. 8, and the diagonal distance, denoted by " D. D.," from the other frog is 26 feet.

In Table No. 6 we find that the curvature of the lead of the No. 10 frog so placed is practically a straight line, and in Table No. 5 that the curvature of the No. 8 is $15\frac{1}{2}$ degrees.

Care should, therefore, be taken not to have the curvature of the inside frog too sharp.

TABLE No. 25.

DIAGONAL DISTANCES BETWEEN FROG POINTS WHEN THE LINE IS STRAIGHT BETWEEN THEM.

4 feet 8½ inch and 4 feet 9 inch gauges.

2-DEGREE CURVE.

FROG ON OUTSIDE OF CURVE.	6 Ft. 6 In.		6 Ft. 9 In.		7 Ft. o In.		7 Ft. 3 In.		7 Ft. 5 In.		7 Ft. 6 In.		7 Ft. 9 In.		8 Ft. o In.	
No.	Frog. No.	D.D. Ft.In.	Frog. No.	D.D. Ft.In.	Frog. No.	D.D. Ft.In.	Frog. No.	D.D. Ft.In.	Frog. No.	D.D. Ft.In.	Frog. No.	D.D. Ft.In.	Frog. No.	D.D. Ft.In.	Frog. No.	D.D. Ft.In.
6	6	12 2	6	13 6	6	14 11	6	16 3	6	17 2	6	17 9	6	19 1	6	20 7
8	8	15 0	8	16 11	8	18 8	8	20 6	8	21 9	8	22 5	8	24 3	8	26 2
10	9	18 2	9	20 0	9	23 2	9	25 5	9	27 1	9	27 10	9	30 2	9	32 6
12	11	21 8	11	24 5	11	27 2	11	29 11	11	31 9	11	32 8	11	35 4	11	37 11
15	14	26 2	14	29 8	13	32 0	13	36 1	12	38 0	12	39 1	12	42 3	12	45 3

4-DEGREE CURVE.

FROG ON OUTSIDE OF CURVE.	6 Ft. 6 In.		6 Ft. 9 In.		7 Ft. o In.		7 Ft. 3 In.		7 Ft. 5 In.		7 Ft. 6 In.		7 Ft. 9 In.		8 Ft. o In.	
No.	Frog. No.	D.D. Ft.In.	Frog. No.	D.D. Ft.In.	Frog. No.	D.D. Ft.In.	Frog. No.	D.D. Ft.In.	Frog. No.	D.D. Ft.In.	Frog. No.	D.D. Ft.In.	Frog. No.	D.D. Ft.In.	Frog. No.	D.D. Ft.In.
6	6	12 1	6	13 6	6	14 10	6	16 3	6	17 2	6	17 8	6	19 1	6	20 7
8	8	15 4	8	17 4	8	19 1	8	21 0	8	22 1	7	22 8	7	24 6	7	26 3
10	9	18 9	9	21 2	9	23 4	9	25 6	9	26 11	9	27 8	9	29 10	9	32 0
12	11	21 7	11	24 1	10	26 7	10	29 1	10	30 9	10	31 7	10	34 0	9	36 3
15	12	25 9	12	28 9	12	31 8	11	34 3	11	36 3	11	37 1	11	40 0	11	42 6

TABLE No. 25.—Continued.

6-Degree Curve.

Frog on Outside of Curve. No.	6 Ft. 6 In. Frog. D. D.		6 Ft. 9 In. D. D.		7 Ft. 0 In. D. D.		7 Ft. 3 In. D. D.		7 Ft. 5 In. D. D.		7 Ft. 6 In. D. D.		7 Ft. 9 In. D. D.		8 Ft. 0 In. D. D.	
	No.	Ft.In.	No.	Ft.In	No.	Ft.In.	No.	Ft.In	No.	Ft.In.	No.	Ft.In.	No.	Ft.In	No.	Ft.In.
6	6	12 2	6	13 7	6	14 11	6	16 3	6	17 3	6	17 9	6	19 1	6	20 6
8	8	15 6	8	17 3	8	19 1	8	20 11	7	22 2	7	22 9	7	24 5	7	26 1
10	9	13 4	9	20 6	9	22 8	8	24 8	8	26 0	8	26 9	8	28 9	8	30 10
12	10	21 3	10	23 7	10	25 11	10	28 3	9	29 9	9	30 7	9	32 10	9	35 0
15	12	25 10	12	28 8	12	31 7	11	34 3	11	36 1	11	37 0	11	39 9	11	42 3

8-Degree Curve.

Frog on Outside of Curve. No.	6 Ft. 6 In.		6 Ft. 9 In.		7 Ft. 0 In.		7 Ft. 3 In.		7 Ft. 5 In.		7 Ft. 6 In.		7 Ft. 9 In.		8 Ft. 0 In.	
	No.	Ft.In.	No.	Ft.In.	No.	Ft.In.	No.	Ft.In.	No.	Ft.In.	No.	Ft.In	No.	Ft.In	No.	Ft.In.
8	8	14 8	8	16 7	8	18 3	8	20 0	7	21 0	7	21 9	7	23 3	7	25 0
10	9	17 10	9	20 0	9	22 2	8	24 3	8	25 7	8	26 4	8	28 3	8	30 3
12	10	20 3	10	22 8	10	25 2	9	27 5	9	28 11	9	29 8	9	31 10	9	34 0
15	12	24 0	12	26 10	10	29 5	10	31 11	10	33 5	9	34 2	9	36 6	9	38 10

THREE-THROW SWITCHES.

Three-throw switches are of two kinds, viz. :—
1. For turning to opposite sides.
2. For turning to the same side.

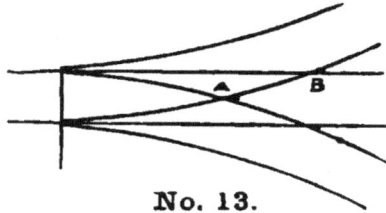

No. 13.

In both cases the main frogs should be opposite each other.

The middle or crotch frog, when turning to opposite sides, is upon the centre line of the main track, and when turning to the same side

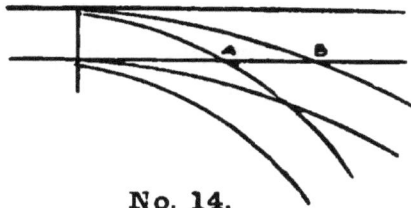

No. 14.

it is upon the line of the frog rail of the main track.

On account of not having frogs of suitable number, it has sometimes been necessary to place one of the main frogs back of the other in turning to the same side, but it should not be done if it can be avoided, on account of the short and insecure guard rail which, in that case, would have to be placed opposite the rear frog, and also because it cannot be made a finished piece of switch work.

The lead of a three-throw in both cases, whether the switch is a point or a stub, is the same as that of a corresponding single turnout, the main-track frog determining its length and curvature.

In a three-throw to the same side, the throw will be the distance the sliding rail moves from the first track to the second ; for the third or extreme inside track it will be twice what it is for one track. Herein is one of the principal objections to a three-throw of this kind, viz., the too great distance the slide rail has to move to conform to or complete the curve of the track farthest away.

In regard to the curvature of the lead, such a combination of frogs should always be used as will give a nearly regular curve from the headblock to the frog point; and the crotch frog, where the curvature is sharp, should be short in length from toe to heel.

The number of the crotch frog theoretically is seven-tenths the number of the main frog, but it is always better to use a frog of the nearest whole number.

In a point three-throw the two main frogs should be opposite each other, but of different numbers, in order to have the point of the switch of the one track at the heel or back of the point of the switch of the other. This can be accomplished by leads of different lengths, and it applies to both cases of three-throws, to the same or to opposite sides.

In a stub three-throw, just as in a single stub turnout, the practicable length of the switch rail should determine what is the highest combination of frogs it is advisable to use, as there would be nothing gained by using frogs which would give a long and easy curve as far as the head-block, when the limited length of the switch rail would greatly increase it beyond that point.

As 27 feet is the length of the longest practicable moving rail, a No. 9 or a No. 10 three-throw should be the maximum and a No. 6 the minimum limit, and this latter only for turning to opposite sides.

In a three-throw to the same side the main frogs should not be less than No. 8 nor greater than No. 10, unless it is upon the outside of a curve, in which case the circumstances should determine the combination of frogs.

When, however, circumstances would warrant using a No. 12 three-throw, the comparative increased curvature of the switch rail should not operate against doing so, if the object is to obtain reduced curvature through the frogs.

The difficulty experienced in putting in a three-throw is to find the position of the point of the crotch frog.

This can be done practically in this manner: Having first set both main frogs and given good line to both outside rails, or as they will be when the three-throw is completed, each of which should be the gauge of the track distant from the crotch frog, find with a tape-line the point between the gauge lines of these two outer rails just lined, where the distance is equal to twice the gauge; at this point place the point of the crotch frog.

Or, having lined the outside rails, as just indicated, use a frog-board, moving it to the point where it will gauge neatly with both outside rails, with perhaps slight adjusting of their line, and at this point place the point of the crotch frog. But the easiest way is to take from Tables Nos. 26 and 27 the distance between the main and the crotch frog, and, measuring along the main rail from A to B, in Diagrams Nos. 13 and 14, place the frog accordingly.

The following tables give the necessary distances for finding the position of the crotch frog by measurement :—

TABLE No. 26.
THREE–THROWS TO OPPOSITE SIDES.

4 FEET 8½ INCH GAUGE.				4 FEET 9 INCH GAUGE.			
Main Frogs.		Crotch Frogs.		Main Frogs.		Crotch Frogs.	
No.	Lead.	No.	Between Points.	No.	Lead.	No.	Between Points.
	Ft. In.		Ft. In.		Ft. In.		Ft. In.
6	56 6	4	16 6	6	57 0	4	16 9
7	65 11	5	19 3	7	66 6	5	19 6
8	75 4	6	22 0	8	76 0	6	22 3
9	84 9	6	24, 9	9	85 6	6	25 0
10	94 2	7	27 6	10	95 0	7	27 9
11	103 7	8	30 3	11	104 6	8	30 6

TABLE No. 27.
THREE–THROWS TO SAME SIDE.

4 FEET 8½ INCH GAUGE.				4 FEET 9 INCH GAUGE.			
Main Frogs.		Crotch Frogs.		Main Frogs.		Crotch Frogs.	
No.	Lead.	No.	Between Points.	No.	Lead.	No.	Between Points.
	Ft. In.		Ft. In.		Ft. In.		Ft. In.
6	56 6	4	16 6	6	57 0	4	16 9
7	65 11	5	19 3	7	66 6	5	19 6
8	75 4	6	22 0	8	76 0	6	22 3
9	84 9	6	24 9	9	85 6	6	25 0
10	94 2	7	27 6	10	95 0	7	27 9
11	103 7	8	30 3	11	104 6	8	30 6

In a three-throw to opposite sides, 4 feet $8\frac{1}{2}$ inch gauge and No. 8 frogs, the crotch frog corresponding is a No. 6, and its distance from either main frog, measured along the main rail to opposite its point, is 22 feet, and it will be upon the centre line of the straight or main track.

For 4 feet 9 inch gauge and No. 10 frogs the corresponding crotch frog is a No. 7, and its distance from main frogs is 27 feet 9 inches. The distance between frog points for all suitable frogs is found in the columns of these tables under the heading "Between Points."

First locate the main frog, and from it measure the distance to the crotch frog, taken from the tables.

In a three-throw to same or opposite sides there is no practical difference in the number of crotch frog and the distance between the frog points, they being the same in both cases, nor is it necessary to have different distances between points for 4 feet $8\frac{1}{2}$ inch and 4 feet 9 inch gauges, as what is suitable to one gauge is just as suitable, practically, to the other, and the same distance can be used for either gauge.

The theoretical number of the crotch frog is obtained by the formula—

$$n = \sqrt{\frac{R'}{2g}}$$

in which n is the number of the crotch frog, g the gauge, and R' the radius of the curve through the crotch frog.

The radius R' of the curve through the crotch frog is obtained by formula—

$$R' = \tfrac{1}{2}(R - \tfrac{1}{2}g)$$

in which R equals the radius of the curve through the main frog and g the gauge.

The theoretical distance between the main and the crotch frog is obtained in this way: First find the distance from the P. C. of the turnout to the point of the crotch frog, which is obtained by either of the following formulas: P. C. to crotch frog, or—

$$l' = \tfrac{g}{2}\sqrt{8n^2 + 1}$$

equals, approximately, 1.414 gn; or P. C. to crotch frog, or—

$$l' = \frac{R}{2c}$$

In these formulas g equals the gauge, n the number of main frog, c the number of crotch frog, and R the radius of the curve, l' being equal to the distance, or lead, to the crotch frog from the point of the curve.

Having obtained the distance from the point of the curve to the crotch frog, subtract it from

the lead of the main frogs. Suppose, for example, the main frogs are No. 10, the crotch
frog No. 7 and the gauge 4 feet 9 inches; the
lead of No. 10 is 95 feet, and the distance, by
the formula, to the crotch frog is 67 feet 3
inches; subtracting this from the lead, we have
27 feet 9 inches as the distance between the
main frog and the crotch frog.

It should not be overlooked that the crotch
frogs available are not usually of an angle or
number exactly corresponding to what they
should be according to theoretical calculation.

For example: In a No. 8 three-throw the
crotch frog is No. $5\frac{66}{100}$, and in a No. 9 it is $6\frac{36}{100}$.
Such fractional numbers, if used at all, are
special frogs, No. 6 being the nearest suitable
standard number, and should be used with
either No. 8 or No. 9.

When the two main frogs in a stub three-
throw are not the same number, generally they
should not be placed opposite each other, but
each should be its lead distance from the head-
block.

The lead of a three-throw is the same as that
of a single turnout having the same number of
frog, and what is true of the turnout as regards
shortening the lead is also true of the three-
throw whenever it may be desirable.

Where a three-throw switch is not an absolute necessity it should not be put in, two singles always being preferable, as two single switches, into which nearly every three-throw can be converted, are safer and more satisfactory.

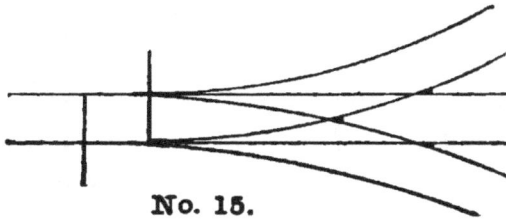

No. 15.

In putting in a three-throw, first determine the position of the main frogs, and from them, by measurement, locate the point of the crotch frog, which can easily be done before any of the frogs are set.

Better and more rapid work can be done by

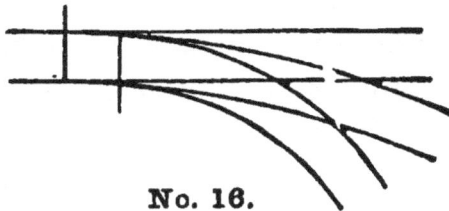

No. 16.

using the tables than by finding the position of the crotch frog practically, provided the measuring is done accurately; at the same time, however, there should be no objection whatever to locating it practically, if it is preferable to do so.

7

As has already been mentioned, it sometimes happens that it is necessary to have a combination of single turnouts, which is equivalent to a three-throw, as shown in Diagrams Nos. 15 and 16.

In a case of this kind it is better to place the main frogs opposite each other. There should be such a difference in their number, and consequently such a difference in their leads, that the point of the switch or the head-block of the shorter lead could be placed at or near the heel of the switch point of the longer lead, the object being to obtain what is equivalent to a three-throw and yet not having the same head-block.

In a stub switch there is no necessity of having frogs of different numbers, as in that case there would be the same head-block and each frog would be the lead distance from the head-block, and, therefore, opposite each other.

Suitable combinations of frogs and distances between points for cases, shown in Diagrams Nos. 15 and 16, are given in the following tables:—

TABLE No. 28.

For 4 feet 8½ inch and 4 feet 9 inch Gauges.

Three-throws to opposite sides.

Frogs.		Distance Between Frog Points.		From Centre Line.
Main.	Crotch.			
No.	No.	Feet.	Inches.	Inches.
10 and 8	6	23	6	2½
11 and 9	7	27	3	2½

To same side.

10 and 8	6	24	8	2½
11 and 9	7	27	6	2½

In the case of a three-throw to opposite sides for these combinations of frogs, the point of the crotch frog will not be upon the centre line between the rails of the main track, but will be about $2\frac{1}{2}$ inches from the centre line, and always upon that side nearer the main frog of the higher number.

For example: It will be upon the side nearer the No. 11 frog in a combination of Nos. 11, 9, and 7, and upon the side nearer the No. 10 in a 10, 8, and 6 combination.

When the main frogs are of the same number and opposite each other, the point of the crotch frog is always exactly half way between the rails, or upon the centre line of the track.

The arrangement of turnouts at the end of a yard, as shown below, is called a "ladder."

It is the most simple and practicable method of connecting yard tracks, the point of all the frogs being at the intersection A of the frog rail of the parallel yard tracks with the frog rail of the ladder track, forming a series of single turnouts from a straight line.

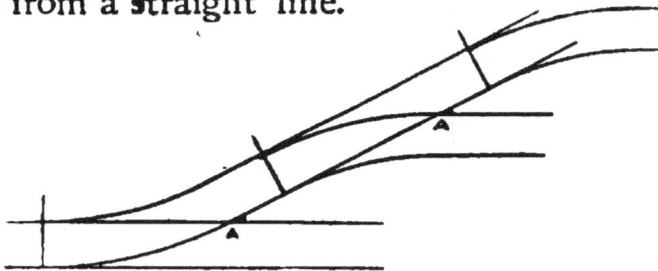

No. 17.

All the yard tracks need not be the same distance apart, although it is better that they should be so ; but they must be parallel.

All the frogs must be of the same number, and the direction of the ladder track must exactly correspond to the angle of the first frog in it.

The principal difficulties to be encountered in the work of putting in a ladder are : *First*, to obtain its correct direction; that is, to mark or stake out upon the ground the line of the angle of the frogs to be used; and, *Second*, to find the location of the points of all the frogs on that line.

When it can be done, where three or four tracks are to be so connected, it is better to have the services of an engineer with an instrument to give the direction of the ladder, but if that is impossible, by following the directions on page 102, any trackman can do it well enough himself. The mistake which is usually made by trackmen is, that having put in the first turn-out or switch of the ladder, they continue with the others, lining them in with the first one, and, by the time three or four have been put in, the ladder is invariably found to be out of line, and it becomes more so as the number of frogs in it increases.

The location of the points of the frogs in a ladder can be ascertained theoretically by calculating the distance between them, and, beginning with the first frog, measuring the distance along the frog rail of the ladder, and locating each frog in order by measurement. That is the easiest and best way to do it. It can also be obtained practically as explained on page 109. Either way, if done accurately, will be satisfactory.

The distance between the frog points in a
ladder will vary according to the distance the
parallel tracks are apart ; and, as it simplifies the
work, so far as possible all the tracks should be
a uniform distance apart.

The Tables, Nos. 30 and 31, give the calculated distance between the points of the frogs in a
ladder for distances between the gauge lines of
the parallel tracks from 6 feet 6 inches to 8 feet,
and can be used in locating the frogs by measurement.   The diagram below shows how to obtain
the direction of a ladder track.

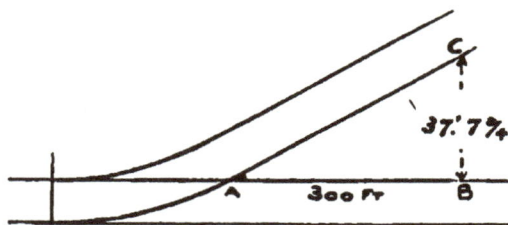

No. 18.

To mark upon the ground the direction of the
frog rail of a ladder, as from A to C, first decide
upon the location of the point of the first frog, as
at A.   This frog we will suppose to be a No. 8 ;
all the frogs in the ladder should, therefore, be
No. 8.

By referring to Table No. 29, we find that for
a No. 8 frog the distance from the straight or
main track to the gauge line of the frog rail of
the ladder opposite a point B, 300 feet from the

point of the first frog at A, is 37 feet 7¾ inches, as shown in the diagram.

Measure 300 feet from the point of the frog, and exactly at a right angle from the gauge line of the rail at B measure 37 feet 7¾ inches to C. C will be a point on the gauge line of the frog rail of a No. 8 ladder. Two points on the line of the ladder will thus be established, one at A and the other at C.

Drive a stake at C and place a tack in it exactly 37 feet 7¾ inches from the gauge of the rail at B, and stretch a string from the point of frog at A and fasten it to the tack in the stake at C. If done accurately, the direction of the string will be the direction of the No. 8 ladder, and the angle that of a No. 8 frog.

Any other of the distances in the table, measured from the points at 100 to 500 feet from the point of the first frog, will give the same direction as that measured at the 300-foot point. If all the measurements in the table were made in the same manner as that from B to C, the stakes at each point would be in the same straight line.

If the ladder is to connect with a number of yard tracks the measurement should be taken from the farthest or 500-foot point, because the line giving the direction of the ladder should be as long as possible.

To insure accuracy, it should be observed, before any offset measurements are made, that the straight track in which the first frog is placed is in good alignment with the remainder of the tangent beyond the point opposite where the end of the ladder will be.

A carpenter's iron square, or a large wooden square, should be used to obtain the right angle in measuring from the straight track, as at B, to the ladder line at C.

A good metallic tape-line, a new one preferred, should be used and the measurements made very accurately.

To further insure accuracy, it is well to take measurements from two points and test them until they agree and are in the same ladder line.

The offset measurements could be made for a No. 8 ladder from the 200 and 400-foot points, and would be 25 feet 1⅛ inches and 50 feet 2⅜ inches, respectively, taken from Table No. 29.

TABLE No. 29.

SHOWING DISTANCES BY WHICH THE DIRECTION OF THE FROG RAIL OF LADDER CAN BE OBTAINED AND LAID OUT UPON THE GROUND FOR FROGS FROM No. 6 TO No. 12 FOR ANY GAUGE.

Frog No.	Distance from Straight Track to Gauge Line of Frog Rail of Ladder at									
	100 Feet.		200 Feet.		300 Feet.		400 Feet.		500 Feet.	
	Ft.	In.	Ft.	In.	Ft.	In.	Ft.	In.	Ft.	In.
6	16	9⅜	33	6¾	50	4¼	67	1⅝	83	11
7	14	4¼	28	8⅝	43	1	57	5¼	71	9½
8	12	6⅝	25	1⅛	37	7¾	50	2⅜	62	9
9	11	1¾	22	3½	33	5⅛	44	6⅞	55	8⅝
10	10	0⅜	20	0⅝	30	1	40	1¼	50	1⅝
11	9	1⅜	18	2⅝	27	4	36	5¼	45	6⅝
12	8	4⅛	16	8⅜	25	0½	33	4¾	41	8⅞

TO FIND THE LOCATION OF THE FROG POINTS IN A LADDER TRACK.

After having established the direction of the ladder track, the next thing is to find the position of the frogs in it. This will depend upon the number or angle of the frog and the distance the parallel tracks are apart.

The best way to do is to locate the frogs by measurement, calculating the distance between the points, and then, beginning with the first frog, as at A, if all the frogs are the same distance apart (which they should be), the distance between the points can be measured and the position of each frog known exactly.

This calculated distance is obtained by using the formula: $c = \frac{a}{Sin.\,A}$ which means that the distance A to B in the diagram, or from the point of one frog to the point of the other, is equal to the distance between the parallel tracks divided by the Sine of the frog angle.

The distances in the following tables for 4 feet $8\frac{1}{2}$ inch and 4 feet 9 inch gauges, and for distances between gauge lines of parallel tracks

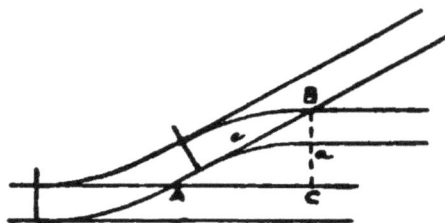

No. 19.

from 6 feet 6 inches to 8 feet, are calculated by this formula.

Suppose it is desired to know the distance between frog points in a No. 9 ladder, gauge 4 feet $8\frac{1}{2}$ inches, and tracks 7 feet between gauge lines.

In Table No. 30, opposite No. 9 frog, and under 7 feet 0 inches, 105 feet $8\frac{1}{2}$ inches is found to be the distance desired.

Also, what is the distance between frog points in a No. 8 ladder, gauge 4 feet 9 inches, and tracks 7 feet 5 inches apart ? See page 109.

TABLE No. 30.

DISTANCE BETWEEN FROG POINTS IN A LADDER TRACK.

4 feet 8½ inch Gauge.

FROG No.	DISTANCE BETWEEN FROG POINTS when DISTANCE BETWEEN TRACKS is—							
	6 Ft. 6 In.	6 Ft. 9 In.	7 Ft. 0 In.	7 Ft. 3 In.	7 Ft. 5 In.	7 Ft. 6 In.	7 Ft. 9 In.	8 Ft. 0 In.
	Ft. In.	Ft. In.	Ft. In.	Ft. In.	Ft. In.	Ft. In.	Ft. In.	Ft. In.
6	67 8¾	69 2¾	70 8¾	72 3-	73 3	73 9	75 3⅛	76 9¼
7	78 10¼	80 7½	82 4½	84 1½	85 3½	85 10¾	87 8	89 5
8	90 0¼	92 0¼	94 0¼	96 0½	97 4½	98 0½	100 0¾	102 0¾
9	101 2½	103 5¼	105 8½	107 11⅞	109 5½	110 2¾	112 5¾	114 8¾
10	112 4½	114 10¾	117 4½	119 10¾	121 6¾	122 4¾	124 10¾	127 4½
11	123 7¼	126 4⅛	129 1	131 10¾	133 8	134 7½	137 4½	140 1½
12	134 9	137 9	140 9	143 9	145 9	146 9	149 9	152 9½

TABLE No. 31.

Distance Between Frog Points in a Ladder Track.

4 feet 9 inch Gauge.

Frog No.	Distance Between Frog Points when Distance Between Tracks is—															
	6 Ft. 6 In.		6 Ft. 9 In.		7 Ft. 0 In.		7 Ft. 3 In.		7 Ft. 5 In.		7 Ft. 6 In.		7 Ft. 9 In.		8 Ft. 0 In.	
	Ft.	In.	Ft.	In.	Ft.	In.	Ft.	In.	Ft.	In.	Ft.	In.	Ft.	In.	Ft.	In.
6	67	11¾	69	6¾	70	11⅞	72	6	73	6	74	0⅛	75	6¼	77	0⅜
7	79	1¾	80	11	82	8¼	84	5¼	85	7½	86	2¼	87	11½	89	8½
8	90	4¼	92	4¼	94	4¼	96	4½	97	8¾	98	4½	100	1¾	102	4¾
9	101	6½	103	10¼	106	1	108	4¼	109	10	110	7¼	112	10¼	115	1½
10	112	9¼	115	3⅜	117	9¾	120	3⅝	122	0	122	10¼	125	4¼	127	10¾
11	124	1	126	9¼	129	7	132	7½	134	1¾	135	1	137	10¼	140	7
12	135	3	138	3	141	3	144	3	146	3	147	3	150	3½	153	3

In Table No. 31, opposite No. 8 frog, and under 7 feet 5 inches, it is found to be 97 feet 8¾ inches.

In using the distances in these tables, measurements should always be taken between the theoretical frog points, not the blunt points, unless allowance has been made in measuring from the first frog, in which event measurements may be made between the blunt points.

The frog points can also be found practically, but not so easily, by using a string and finding the intersection of the parallel tracks with the line of the ladder track in this way:—

To whatever distance the tracks are apart add the gauge of the track. For example: If they are 7 feet 3 inches and the gauge is 4 feet 9 inches, the table distance between gauge lines would be 12 feet. Drive a stake upon each side of the ladder track, and place a tack in it 12 feet from the gauge of the main-track rail and stretch a string between them.

The string will correspond to the gauge line of the parallel track, and its intersection with the string giving the direction of the ladder will be the frog point.

For the second parallel track the distance will be twice 12, or 24 feet, and for the third, 36 feet, and so on, adding 12 feet for each additional track.

If done accurately, the points so obtained will be the same as those obtained from the tables.

A ladder composed of No. 8, 9, or 10 frogs is the most practicable.

A three-throw ladder is not impracticable, but it is not advisable, as a single ladder is much superior.

SWITCH TIMBER.

It is too much to give here a bill of timber for every variation possible in a turnout or cross-over. The bills which are given are for frogs from Nos. 6 to 15, for the theoretical lead, for 4 feet 8½ inch or 4 feet 9 inch gauges, and distance between centres of switch timber 22 inches. They are suitable to cross-ties 8 feet 6 inches long, and, in the case of cross-overs, are for distances between gauge lines of parallel tracks from 6 feet 6 inches to 8 feet.

These bills can easily be changed to suit any variation from these conditions as a basis. For example: For a short lead, by omitting a certain number of the pieces near the switch point.

The number of pieces in any bill depends upon the distance apart it is necessary to have them and also upon the lead.

Generally, for large hewn timber the distance between centres should be about 24 inches; for timber sawed upon the four sides, and having 10 inches face, it should be about 22 inches; and for small timber, having 8 inches face, it should be about 20 inches. About the best size for switch timber is 7 inches thick, 10 inches face, and distance between centres of pieces 22 inches, or about 12 inches apart. The thickness should be the same as that of cross-ties, and should not be less than 6½ nor more than 7 inches.

Knowing the distance between centres, the number of pieces between the switch and the frog point can be determined by reducing the lead to inches and dividing it by the distance between centres. For example : A lead of 76 feet for a No. 8 frog is equal to 912 inches; dividing 912 by 22 inches, the distance between centres, 41 pieces are found to be required between the head-block and the frog point. It is impossible to space the timber the exact distance apart on account of the rail joints, but the number of pieces obtained in this manner, disregarding the joints, is sufficient for a good bill.

The length for each piece is more difficult to obtain, if it is desired to make the bill conform to the line of the turnout curve. One way which will give regularly increasing lengths, not conforming to the curve, however, is to reduce to inches the difference between the lengths of the cross-tie at the head-block and the switch-tie under the frog point, and divide this difference by the number of pieces necessary between the head-block and the frog point. The length so obtained should be added to each piece, begin-

ning with the 8 or 8½ foot cross-tie at the head-
block, and thus increase to the proper length under the frog point and also to the last long piece.

If, for example, the piece under the frog is 13
feet 3 inches and the cross-ties are 8 feet 6 inches
long, the difference between them is 4 feet 9
inches, or 57 inches. Fifty-seven inches divided
by 41, the number of pieces between the head-
block and the frog, give about 1½ inches difference, which should be added to each piece so as
to increase in 41 pieces from 8 feet 6 inches to
13 feet 3 inches.

When all the pieces are in position the pro-
jecting ends can be chopped off so as to conform
to the turnout curve, if it is so desired.

But to make a bill conform to the turnout
curve, the formula, or way of calculating the
stub lead, on page 30, can be used, as by it the
position of certain pieces can be calculated, and
having it and also their length, the remaining
pieces can be easily placed between them. If, by
assuming that every 6 inches difference in the
length of the pieces is equal to the throw of a
stub switch, the piece which belongs at each
throw will be a distance from the frog point
equal to the stub lead for the same throw; that
is, if the first throw is 6 inches, the second 12
inches, the third 18 inches, and so on, until the

8

throw nearly equals the gauge, the position of each piece can be determined, and, by adding the intervening pieces, the bill can be completed.

For cross-ties 8½ feet long, the following table gives the throw and length of the corresponding piece:—

Where the throw is		the piece is	
"	6 inches,	9	feet long.
"	1 foot	9½	"
"	1½ feet	10	"
"	2 "	10½	"
"	2½ "	11	"
"	3 "	11½	"
"	3½ "	12	"
"	4 "	12½	"

If the cross-ties are 8 instead of 8½ feet long the pieces will be 6 inches less. At the frog point the length of the piece is equal to the 4 feet 9 inch gauge added to the length of the cross tie, 8½ feet, making 13 feet 3 inches, and a cross-tie 8 feet long added to 4 feet 9 inches is 12 feet 9 inches. This method should be used only as a help in making a bill which curves with the turnout.

It is hardly worth while to spend much time making out with exactness a bill of timber, as it is rarely, if ever, cut according to the bill, and to have a finished piece of work it is invariably necessary to chop off the ends to a certain length.

The governing pieces are the head-block, generally about 12 feet long, the frog-tie, that is, the piece under the frog point, 13 feet 3 inches long for cross-ties 8 feet 6 inches, and 12 feet 9 inches long for cross-ties 8 feet long, and the last long piece back of the frog, which is about 16 feet or 16 feet 6 inches long.

If these governing pieces are first placed in their proper position, all the other intervening ones will naturally fall into their places when putting in the timber.

By deducting 6 inches from each piece, these bills for 8½ feet cross-ties can be changed to suit cross-ties 8 feet long.

The number of pieces back of the frog is optional, about 16 feet being a good length for the last long piece.

Divide the distance, in inches, between the frog point and last long tie by the distance between centres, to ascertain the number of pieces back of the frog point.

The following bills are for the theoretical lead, 8½ feet cross-ties and about 22 inches between centres.

If a shorter lead is used, it is necessary to omit some of the pieces, not back of the frog, but beyond the heel of the switch, where, on account of the length of the theoretical lead, the turnout curve is flat.

No complete bills are given for cross-overs, yet enough is given in Tables Nos. 32 and 33 to enable a bill to be easily made. First ascertain from the tables, according to the distance the tracks are apart, how many long pieces are required, and also the length of the last short piece. The single bill for the corresponding frog up to the last short piece can be used to complete the cross-over bill.

BILL FOR NO. 6, SINGLE.

Gauges, 4 feet 8½ inches and 4 feet 9 inches.
Theoretical lead, 57 feet.
Between centres, 22 inches.
Cross-tie, 8½ feet.

Pcs.	Ft.	In.	Ft.	In.	Ft.	In.	Ft.	In.	Ft.	In.	Ft.	In.
	12	0	9	0	10	0	11	3	12	9	14	4
4	8	6	9	2	10	2	11	6	13	0	14	8
	8	7	9	4	10	4	11	9	13	3	15	0
	8	8	9	6	10	6	12	0	13	6	15	4
	8	9	9	8	10	9	12	3	13	9	15	8
	8	10	9	10	11	0	12	6	14	0	16	0

For stub lead, omit the first eight or ten pieces under the switch.

For 8 feet cross-tie, use pieces 6 inches shorter and omit the last two pieces.

The piece which belongs under the frog point is 13 feet 3 inches for 8½ feet cross-tie, and 12 feet 9 inches for 8 feet cross-tie.

For No. 7, Single.

Gauges, 4 feet 8½ inches and 4 feet 9 inches.
Theoretical lead, 66 feet 6 inches.
Between centres, 22 inches.
Cross-tie, 8½ feet.

Pcs.	Ft.	In.	Ft.	In.	Ft.	In.	Ft.	In.	Ft.	In.	Ft.	In.
	12	0	9	1	10	2	11	6	13	6	15	6
4	8	6	9	2	10	4	11	9	13	9	15	9
	8	7	9	3	10	6	12	0	14	0	16	0
	8	8	9	4	10	8	12	3	14	3	16	3
	8	9	9	6	10	10	12	6	14	6	16	6
	8	10	9	8	11	0	12	9	14	9		
	8	11	9	10	11	2	13	0	15	0		
	9	0	10	0	11	4	13	3	15	3		

For stub lead, omit the first eight or ten pieces.

For 8 feet cross-tie, use pieces 6 inches shorter and omit the last four pieces.

For No. 8, Single.

Gauges, 4 feet 8½ inches and 4 feet 9 inches.
Theoretical lead, 76 feet.
Between centres, 22 inches.
Cross-tie, 8½ feet.

Pcs.	Ft.	In.	Ft.	In.	Ft.	In.	Ft.	In.	Ft.	In.	Ft.	In.	Ft.	In.
	12	0	9	0	9	7	10	6	11	9	13	3	15	0
6	8	6	9	1	9	8	10	8	12	0	13	6	15	3
	8	7	9	2	9	10	10	10	12	3	13	9	15	6
	8	8	9	3	10	0	11	0	12	6	14	0	15	9
	8	9	9	4	10	1	11	2	12	9	14	3	16	0
	8	10	9	5	10	2	11	4	13	0	14	6	16	3
	8	11	9	6	10	4	11	6	13	1	14	9	16	6

For 72 feet short lead, omit the two pieces near the switch, but not under it.

For stub lead, omit the first eight or ten pieces.

For 8 feet cross-tie, use pieces 6 inches shorter and omit the last five pieces.

FOR NO. 9, SINGLE.

Gauges, 4 feet 8½ and 4 feet 9 inches.
Theoretical lead, 85 feet 6 inches.
Between centres, 22 inches.
Cross-tie, 8½ feet.

Pcs.	Ft.	In.	Pcs.	Ft.	In.	Ft.	In.	Ft.	In.	Ft.	In.	Ft.	In.
	12	0	2	9	2	10	2	11	6	13	0	15	3
6	8	6	2	9	3	10	4	11	8	13	3	15	6
	8	7		9	4	10	6	11	10	13	6	15	8
	8	8		9	5	10	7	12	0	13	9	15	10
	8	9		9	6	10	8	12	2	14	0	16	0
	8	10		9	7	10	10	12	4	14	3	16	3
	8	11		9	8	11	0	12	6	14	6	16	6
2	9	0		9	10	11	2	12	8	14	9		
2	9	1		10	0	11	4	12	10	15	0		

For 76 feet 6 inches short lead, omit four of the duplicate pieces longer than 9 feet.

For stub lead, omit first twelve or fourteen pieces.

For 8 feet cross-tie, use pieces 6 inches shorter and omit the last five pieces.

·FOR NO. 10, SINGLE.

Gauges, 4 feet 8½ and 4 feet 9 inches.
Theoretical lead, 95 feet.
Between centres, 22 inches.
Cross-tie, 8½ feet.

Pcs.	Ft.	In.	Pcs.	Ft.	In.	Ft.	In.	Ft.	In.	Ft.	In.	Ft.	In.
	12	0	2	9	3	10	1	11	4	13	0	15	2
5	8	6	2	9	4	10	2	11	6	13	1	15	4
	8	7		9	5	10	3	11	8	13	3	15	6
	8	8		9	6	10	4	11	10	13	6	15	8
	8	9		9	7	10	6	12	0	13	9	15	10
	8	10		9	8	10	8	12	2	14	0	16	0
	8	11		9	9	10	10	12	4	14	3	16	2
	9	0		9	10	11	0	12	6	14	6	16	4
2	9	1		9	11	11	1	12	8	14	9	16	6
2	9	2		10	0	11	2	12	10	15	0		

For 85 feet short lead, omit the five duplicate pieces longer than 9 feet.

For stub lead, omit the first sixteen or seventeen pieces.

For 8 feet cross-tie, use pieces 6 inches shorter and omit last six pieces.

FOR NO. 11, SINGLE.

Gauges, 4 feet 8½ and 4 feet 9 inches.
Lead, 104 feet 6 inches.
Between centres, 22 inches.
Cross-tie, 8½ feet.

Pcs.	Ft. In.	Pcs.	Ft. In.	Ft. In.	Ft. In.	Ft. In.	Ft. In.
	12 0	2	9 4	10 4	11 8	13 6	15 4
6	8 6	2	9 5	10 6	11 10	13 8	15 6
	8 7	2	9 6	10 7	12 0	13 10	15 8
	8 8		9 7	10 8	12 2	14 0	15 10
	8 9		9 8	10 10	12 4	14 2	16 0
	8 10		9 9	11 0	12 6	14 4	16 2
	8 11		9 10	11 1	12 8	14 6	16 4
2	9 0		9 11	11 2	12 10	14 8	16 6
2	9 1		10 0	11 4	13 0	14 10	
2	9 2		10 2	11 6	13 1	15 0	
2	9 3		10 3	11 7	13 3	15 2	

For 88 feet short lead, omit the seven duplicate pieces.

For 8 feet cross-tie, use pieces 6 inches shorter
and omit the last six pieces.

FOR NO. 12, SINGLE.

Gauges, 4 feet 8½ and 4 feet 9 inches.
Lead, 114 feet.
Between centres, 22 inches.
Cross-tie, 8½ feet.

Pcs.	Ft. In.	Pcs.	Ft. In.	Ft. In.	Ft. In.	Ft. In.	Ft. In.
	12 0	2	9 4	10 4	11 8	13 4	15 2
6	8 6	2	9 5	10 6	11 10	13 6	15 4
	8 7	2	9 6	10 7	12 0	13 8	15 6
	8 8	2	9 7	10 8	12 2	13 10	15 8
	8 9	2	9 8	10 9	12 4	14 0	15 10
	8 10		9 9	10 10	12 6	14 2	16 0
	8 11		9 10	11 0	12 8	14 4	16 2
2	9 0		9 11	11 1	12 10	14 6	16 4
2	9 1		10 0	11 2	13 0	14 8	16 6
2	9 2		10 2	11 4	13 1	14 10	
2	9 3		10 3	11 6	13 3	15 0	

For 96 feet short lead, omit the nine duplicate pieces longer than 9 feet.

For stub lead, omit the first twenty pieces, including duplicates, except those under switch.

For 8 feet cross-tie, use pieces 6 inches shorter and omit the last six pieces.

FOR NO. 15, SINGLE.

Gauges, 4 feet 8½ inches and 4 feet 9 inches.
Lead, 142 feet 6 inches.
Between centres, 22 inches.
Cross-tie, 8½ feet.

Pcs.	Ft.	In.	Pcs.	Ft.	In.	Ft.	In.	Ft.	In.	Ft.	In.	Ft.	In.
	12	0	2	9	7	10	9	11	11	13	2	14	4
6	8	6	2	9	8	10	10	12	0	13	3	14	6
	8	7		9	9	10	11	12	1	13	4	14	8
	8	8		9	10	11	0	12	2	13	5	14	10
	8	9		9	11	11	1	12	3	13	6	15	0
	8	10		10	0	11	2	12	4	13	7	15	2
	8	11		10	1	11	3	12	6	13	8	15	4
2	9	0		10	2	11	4	12	7	13	9	15	6
2	9	1		10	3	11	5	12	8	13	10	15	8
2	9	2		10	4	11	6	12	9	13	11	15	10
2	9	3		10	5	11	7	12	10	14	0	16	0
2	9	4		10	6	11	8	12	11	14	1	16	2
2	9	5		10	7	11	9	13	0	14	2	16	4
2	9	6		10	8	11	10	13	1	14	3	16	6

For 120 feet short lead, omit nine duplicate pieces longer than 9 feet.

For 8 feet cross-tie, use pieces 6 inches shorter and omit last six pieces.

To make a bill for No. 8 cross-over, if the distance between the gauge lines is 7 feet 6 inches, and to suit 8 feet 6 inch cross-tie, look in Table No. 32, and under 7 feet 6 inches, 12 feet 3 inches is found to be the length of the last short piece and 20 feet 9 inches the length of the long pieces. In Table No. 33, for No. 8

cross-over, under 7 feet 6 inches, we find that 21 long pieces are necessary.

As 12 feet 3 inches is the length of the last short piece, all the pieces preceding it in the bill for No. 8 single, on page 117, are necessary to complete this bill for one end of the cross-over. Add these same pieces for the other end, observing to omit certain pieces, as directed, if a short lead is used. The number of pieces for this No. 8 cross-over are 74 short and 21 long, or a total of 95. If the distance between gauge lines is 7 feet 5 inches, use the bill for 7 feet 6 inches.

TABLE No. 32.

TIMBER FOR CROSS-OVERS.

LENGTH OF LAST SHORT PIECE.

CROSS-TIE.		DISTANCE BETWEEN GAUGE LINES.						
		6 ft. 6 in.	6 ft. 9 in.	7 ft. 0 in.	7 ft. 3 in.	7 ft. 6 in.	7 ft. 9 in.	8 ft. 0 in.
Ft.	In.	Ft. In.	Ft. In.	Ft. In.	Ft. In.	Ft. In.	Ft. In.	Ft. In.
8	0	11 3	12 0	12 3	12 6	12 9	12 0	13 3
8	6	11 3	11 6	11 9	12 0	12 3	12 6	12 9

LENGTH OF LONG PIECES.

8	0	19 3	19 6	19 9	20 0	20 3	20 6	20 9
8	6	19 9	20 0	20 3	20 6	20 9	21 0	21 3

TABLE No. 33.
NUMBER OF LONG PIECES IN No. 6 CROSS-OVER.

CROSS-TIE.		DISTANCE BETWEEN GAUGE LINES.						
		6 ft. 6 in.	6 ft. 9 in.	7 ft. 0 in.	7 ft. 3 in.	7 ft. 6 in.	7 ft. 9 in.	8 ft. 0 in.
Ft.	In.	Feet.	Feet.	Feet.	Feet.	Feet.	Feet.	Feet.
8	0	18	17	16	15	14	13	12
8	6	22	21	20	19	18	17	16

No. 7 CROSS-OVER.

8	0	19	18	17	16	15	14	13
8	6	23	22	21	20	19	18	17

No. 8 CROSS-OVER.

8	0	22	21	20	19	19	17	16
8	6	25	24	23	22	21	20	19

No. 9 CROSS-OVER.

8	0	25	24	23	21	19	17	16
8	6	28	27	26	25	24	23	22

No. 10 CROSS-OVER.

8	0	28	26	24	23	22	20	18
8	6	32	30	28	27	26	25	24

No. 11 CROSS-OVER.

8	0	30	28	26	24	22	20	19
8	6	36	34	32	30	28	26	25

TABLE No. 33 (Continued).

NUMBER OF LONG PIECES IN No. 12 CROSS-OVER.

CROSS-TIE.		DISTANCE BETWEEN GAUGE LINES.						
		6 ft. 6 in.	6 ft. 9 in.	7 ft. 0 in.	7 ft. 3 in.	7 ft. 6 in.	7 ft. 9 in.	8 ft. 0 in.
Ft.	In.	Feet.	Feet.	Feet.	Feet.	Feet.	Feet.	Feet.
8	0	32	30	28	27	25	24	22
8	6	39	37	35	32	30	28	26

No. 15 CROSS-OVER.

8	0	40	38	36	34	32	30	28
8	6	50	47	44	41	38	36	34

If the cross-ties are 8 feet long, the length of the long pieces is 20 feet 3 inches, 19 of which, instead of 21, are necessary. The last short piece being 12 feet 9 inches, the number of short pieces are 76, or a total of 95, the same as for the $8\frac{1}{2}$ feet cross-tie.

A bill for any other frog and distance between gauge lines of parallel tracks can be obtained in the same manner.

BILL FOR THREE-THROW.

Having a bill of timber for any single turnout for any frog, it can easily be converted into one for a corresponding three-throw by subtracting one-half the length of the 8 or 8 feet 6 inch cross-tie from any piece of timber in the single bill and multiplying the difference by two. For example: For a No. 8 three-throw the length of the pieces under the frog in the single bill for 8 feet cross-tie is 12 feet 9 inches; subtracting 4 feet, or one-half the cross-tie, makes a difference of 8 feet 9 inches; twice 8 feet 9 inches are 17 feet 6 inches, or the length of the piece under the frog in a three-throw.

For 8 feet 6 inch cross-tie, the frog piece is 13 feet 3 inches; subtracting 4 feet 3 inches, the difference is 9 feet, and multiplying by 2, we have 18 feet as the length of the piece under the frog in a three-throw.

The same is true for any other pieces.

The length of the piece under the point of the crotch frog is the same as that of the piece under the frog of the single bill, which is equal to the gauge of the track added to the length of the cross-tie, or 4 feet 9 inches and 8 feet 6 inches, making 13 feet 3 inches for 8 feet 6 inch cross-tie, and 12 feet 9 inches for 8 feet cross-tie.

If the three-throw is a stub, the single bill for the stub lead is to be changed, not the bill for the point lead.

CURVES.

The alignment of a railroad is made up of curves and tangents, tangent meaning a straight line. The names of curves most generally used are Regular, Compound, and Reverse.

The flattened end of a curve is known as Elastic, Parabolic, Transition, and Spiral—all being practically the same.

A REGULAR CURVE.

A Regular Curve is one whose curvature remains the same as to degree from beginning to

No. 20.

end. The point where it begins is denoted as the P. C., or point of curvature, and where it ends as the P. T., or point of tangency.

This diagram represents a 4-degree curve; if it remains a 4-degree for its entire length, A to B, it is a regular curve, because its curvature neither increases nor diminishes; but if it is for a portion of its length 4 degrees and for the remainder changes one or more times to any other degree than 4, it is a Compound Curve.

(127)

A COMPOUND CURVE.

A Compound Curve is made up of a number of curves of different degrees, the number not being limited, and so connected as to form a continuous curve, as shown below.

Its curvature, therefore, increases or diminishes, but its general direction remains the same. In Diagram No. 21 it may begin, say a 4, then

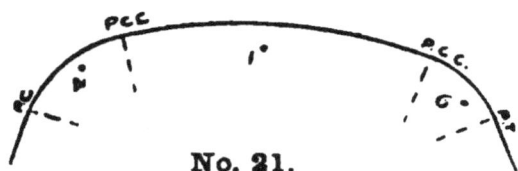

No. 21.

change to a 1, then to a 6, where it ends with the tangent. It may begin of any desirable degree of curvature and be composed of any desirable number of curves, every change of which is denoted at the point where the change begins by P. C. C., or point of compound curvature, the beginning being denoted by P. C. and the end by P. T., just as in a regular curve.

A REVERSE CURVE.

A Reverse Curve is one in which the curvature reverses, or changes from one direction to the opposite, from right to left or left to right, the point at which it reverses being denoted by P. R. C., or point of reverse curvature, as in the diagram below.

The two curves so reversing may be both regular or both compound, or one compound and the other regular.

No. 22.

The difference between a compound and a reverse curve is this : A compound changes as to degree of curvature, and a reverse changes as to direction. Two curves similar to a reverse, having a short piece of tangent or straight line between them, are sometimes erroneously called a reverse. Practically, they may be, but to be a genuine reverse they must reverse at a point and have no straight line whatever between them. There is, however, no objection to treating a case where there is a short tangent practically as a reverse.

THE DEGREE OF CURVATURE.

The measure of the curvature, or the sharp-
ness of a curve, is called the degree of curvature.

As what is meant by the term "degree" is
beyond the clear understanding of any one not
well advanced in mathematics, no attempt will
be made to explain it, beyond the idea that may

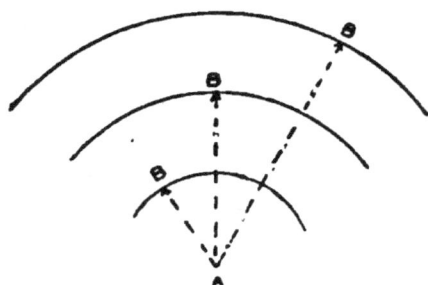

No. 23.

be conveyed by explaining what is called the
radius.

THE RADIUS.

If a string of any convenient length be secured
at one end, at the surface of the ground, to a
stake, and, with a sharp stick fastened to the
other end, a curve were described upon the
ground, as shown, the string A B would correspond to the radius.

From the diagram, it is clear that the shorter the string, or radius, the sharper the curve, and, also, the longer the string, or radius, the longer or flatter the curve. To describe a 1-degree curve, the string would have to be 5730 feet long, and a 10-degree curve it would be one-tenth of 5730 feet, or 573 feet. So, to know what the radius of any curve is, divide 5730 by the degree of the curve. The correct radius is 5729 feet 8 inches, but 5730 feet is sufficiently correct and is generally used.

The reason the amount of curvature is expressed as the degree of curvature, is because curves are laid out not in the manner shown, but by means of a surveying instrument upon the curve itself, the different points of which are located or determined by means of degrees which are equal sub-divisions of a circle.

As the trackman's knowledge of curvature is largely by comparison with other curves known to him, a knowledge of what the radius is may convey an idea as to the degree or to the extent which one curve differs from another. The following is a table of degrees with the corresponding radius :—

TABLE No. 34.

DEGREE OF CURVATURE WITH CORRESPONDING RADIUS.

DEGREE.	RADIUS.	DEGREE.	RADIUS.
	Feet.		Feet.
1	5730	11	521
2	2865	12	477
3	1910	13	441
4	1433	14	409
5	1146	15	380
6	955	16	358
7	819	17	338
8	717	18	318
9	637	19	301
10	573	20	286

TO ASCERTAIN THE DEGREE OF CURVATURE.

As a matter of information merely, every fore-man should know the degree of curvature of every curve on his section, and, also, the way to ascertain it. In addition to this, he should know what it is, so as to intelligently determine the proper elevation, the basis of which is a certain amount for every degree of curvature, according to the speed.

To ascertain the degree of any curve, take a fine twine string about 64 or 65 feet long, and about 12 inches from either end tie a knot; from this knot, with the string stretched tight, measure carefully 31 feet and tie another knot; continue this measurement, and 31 feet further tie another knot, the distance between the extreme knots, at A and B, being 62 feet, the intermediate knot being at C, or exactly midway between them, as shown in Diagram No. 24.

At any point upon the curve, hold one of the knots at the end upon the gauge side of the rail head, as at A, and, with the string stretched tight, place the knot at the other end of the string upon a corresponding point, as B, at the gauge side of the rail also.

At the middle knot C, with a foot-rule, measure carefully the distance from the string to a
point on the rail head corresponding to that at
which each end of the string is placed, and the
distance, in inches, from the string to the rail will
be equal, approximately, to the degree of curvature. The distance to the rail at the middle
knot is called the middle ordinate of a chord,
and is sometimes known to foremen as the " middle distance."

The string corresponds to the chord and the
curving rails between the ends of the string cor-

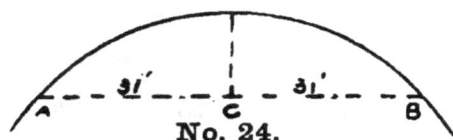

No. 24.

respond to the arc or portion of a circle. According as the string is long or short the middle
ordinate is great or small. In sharp curvature
it is, therefore, greater than in light curvature.

The reason the length of the string between
the extreme knots should be preferably 62 feet
is, that when that length is applied to a 1-de-
gree curve it will give a middle ordinate of 1
inch, and 2 inches for a 2-degree curve, 3 inches
for a 3-degree curve, and so on for any curve.

This method of ascertaining the degree will
not give the degree so accurately as it can be

obtained by an engineer with an instrument, but it can be depended upon as sufficiently accurate for practical purposes, such as for elevating.

Because a string 62 feet long will give a middle ordinate of 1 inch when applied to a 1-degree curve, it does not follow that one just half as long, or 31 feet, will give an ordinate of $\frac{1}{2}$ inch if applied to the same curve.

The length of the string which will give $\frac{1}{2}$ inch on a 1-degree curve is 44 feet.

The following table gives the different lengths of string and the corresponding ordinate, when applied to a 1-degree curve.

TABLE No. 35.

WHEN APPLIED TO A ONE-DEGREE CURVE.

LENGTH OF STRING.	MIDDLE ORDINATE.	LENGTH OF STRING.	MIDDLE ORDINATE.
Feet.	Inches.	Feet.	Inches.
76	1½	49	⅝
69	1¼	44	½
66	1⅛	39	⅜
62	1	31	¼
58	⅞	22	⅛
54	¾		

Some trackmen have been taught, and find it very convenient, to use a 43, 50, or 54-foot string for the same purpose, and it is proper for them to continue to do so if desirable, as the same result can be obtained with a string of any reasonable length. There is, however, an advantage in using the 62-foot length, as it will give an ordinate of 1 inch on a 1-degree curve, and for any curve greater than a 1-degree the ordinate will be as many times greater than 1 inch as the curvature is more than 1 degree.

For example: A 62-foot string will give an ordinate of 3 inches on a 3-degree curve; 6 inches on a 6-degree curve; 20 inches on a 20-degree curve, and so on for any number of degrees, the length of the ordinate always corresponding to the degree. So it may be taken as a safe rule that in every case where a 62-foot string is used the middle ordinate, in inches, corresponds approximately to the degree of curvature.

By reference to Table No. 35, it is seen that a 43, 50, and 54-foot chord or string gives $\frac{1}{2}$, $\frac{5}{8}$, and $\frac{3}{4}$-inch ordinates, respectively, for 1 degree of curvature. To ascertain by these lengths what the curvature of any curve above 1 degree is, it is necessary to divide the ordinate by the fractions of an inch corresponding to those lengths of string. This is more difficult than by using a 62-foot string, which will show at a glance what the degree is.

The ordinate should be measured, not at one place alone, but at several points, before being satisfied as to what the degree is, although generally one measurement should be sufficient to give an idea of what the curvature is.

THE LIMIT OF CURVATURE.

There is a limit to curvature for the economical operation of a railroad, and, while for main track it is desirable not to exceed a curvature of 2 or 3 degrees, it may sometimes be necessary to exceed even 10. Six degrees should be the maximum for main tracks of the standard 4 feet 8½ inch and 4 feet 9 inch gauges. However, sharp main-track curves are unavoidable rather than optional.

In main-track, turnout curves as high as 17 degrees, which curve is suitable to a No. 6 frog, are a doubtful expedient, it not being advisable in any case to exceed the curvature of a No. 8 turnout, or about 9½ degrees, if it can be avoided.

The maximum curvature which can safely be used by a standard road engine, at moderate speed, is about 20 degrees, and this should be the limit. Freight cars and yard or shifting engines, made for sharp curvature, can use with safety from 40 to 60 degrees, according to their construction; but these are extremes, to be avoided as a rule.

TO LINE A CURVE.

Where the centre stakes of a curve are given by the engineer, it is easy to line a curve accurately, but, generally, trackmen have no such assistance, and they have to depend entirely upon the eye for lining their track.

All curves, after a few renewals of cross-ties, are more or less out of line, and have sharp and flat places in them which are very noticeable at full speed. Such spots may not be detected by the eye when lining, but they can be by using a string and measuring the middle ordinate in the same manner as is done to find the degree of curvature.

So long as the middle ordinates are equal, or nearly so, it indicates that the curvature is uniform, but when they vary, that is, increase and decrease frequently, it indicates very bad line, and the greater the difference between them, and the more frequently they change, the worse the alignment. To correct such line, the track should be thrown at such points so that, as far as possible, the ordinates will be nearly equal. A regular curve, whose ordinates are equal, is in perfect line, so far as perfection in railroad work can be attained.

(139)

To ascertain whether a curve is in good line, take a string 62 feet long or of any other reasonable length, and knot it in the manner explained on page 133, and measure the middle ordinates and mark each one with chalk upon the base of the rail at the point where it is measured, beginning at the point of the curve and continuing around the curve, as shown, A to C, B to D, C to E, in the diagram below.

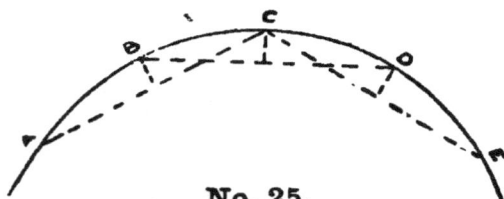

No. 25.

If the length of the string or chord is 62 feet, that will be the distance from A to C, and so on.

From A to B being one-half the length of the string, the ordinate will thus be measured every 31 feet, and by marking it distinctly upon the base of the rail with chalk, it can easily be seen whether or not the curve is in good line. If it is, all the ordinates will be nearly equal ; if it is not, they will vary, and the greater the difference the worse the line.

Write the ordinates upon a piece of paper in the order measured, so that it can be seen at a glance what they are for the whole curve.

Suppose, starting from the beginning of the curve, it should be found that they were nearly uniform, something like as follows: $4\frac{1}{4}$ inches, $4\frac{1}{4}$ inches, $3\frac{3}{4}$ inches, $4\frac{1}{4}$ inches, $4\frac{1}{4}$ inches, $4\frac{1}{4}$ inches. It indicates that the curve is in very fair line, because the ordinates vary but little, and, also, that the curvature is about $4\frac{1}{4}$ degrees, and all that can be done to improve it would be to throw the track towards the high side of the curve a little, to slightly increase the curvature at the place where the ordinate is $3\frac{3}{4}$ inches, which indicates slightly decreased curvature at that ordinate point.

But if the ordinates vary something like this: $4\frac{1}{4}$ inches, $6\frac{1}{8}$ inches, $5\frac{1}{8}$ inches, $5\frac{1}{4}$ inches, $4\frac{1}{4}$ inches, $6\frac{5}{8}$ inches, $4\frac{1}{4}$ inches, 3 inches, it indicates that the curve is not in good line.

To remedy a case where the defect in the alignment is so marked, the foreman must rely upon his exercise of good judgment. Where the ordinates are $6\frac{1}{8}$ and $6\frac{5}{8}$ inches, the track should be lined toward the centre, or inside, of the curve, and the lining carried in both directions, reducing slightly the intervening ordinates so that they all may be uniform.

It is not advisable to throw the track toward the high side at the points where the ordinates are small, unless the difference between them and the next change is considerable and continues for some distance around the curve. In such a case, the sharp places should be lined towards the centre and the flat ones towards the high side of the curve.

After the curve has been thrown for the purpose of correcting the line, begin again at the starting point and measure the ordinates again and mark the length of each upon the base of the rail, having rubbed out the chalk mark first made at the same point.

If the ordinates are found to be equal, or nearly so, then the curve should be satisfactory. If not, then throw it where it is necessary and measure the ordinates again, and continue to throw and measure until it is satisfactory. A little experience will enable the foreman to improve bad curves rapidly and intelligently, although at first the work will be slow, and perhaps tedious and faulty.

What has just been mentioned refers to regular curves. It may happen that after going some distance around the curve the ordinates suddenly increase or decrease, and then continue nearly uniform for the remainder, or for a portion of the remainder, of the curve. For example : Those first measured may be $2\frac{1}{2}$ inches, $2\frac{3}{4}$ inches, $2\frac{1}{4}$ inches, $2\frac{1}{4}$ inches, $2\frac{3}{4}$ inches, 3 inches, and

then change to 5 inches, 5$\frac{1}{2}$ inches, 5$\frac{1}{4}$ inches,
5 inches, 5 inches, 5$\frac{1}{4}$ inches. This would indicate that the curve began about 2$\frac{1}{2}$ degrees and
was then compounded at a certain point to 5
degrees.

Wherever a change like this occurs, and if
beyond where the change occurs the ordinates
are nearly equal, it is fair to presume that it is a
compounded curve. The change from one compound to another should be made gradually so
as to blend, as it were, from the 3 to the 5-degree
curve, or from the 3 to the 5-inch ordinate.

Between the 3 and 5-inch ordinates there
would be a sharp spot, which should not be permitted to remain, and which should be removed
by throwing the track towards the low side until
the ordinates increase gradually from 2$\frac{1}{2}$ to 5
inches.

There should be no such abrupt changes in a
curve, and, ordinarily, any stakes, stones or mon-
uments placed for the permanent marking of the
alignment of the curve where the compounds
are so abrupt, should be disregarded, if, by ad-
hering to them, the track could not be made to
give smooth riding to the train, as, after all, that
is what is desired.

The points or ends of curves thrown to a line
so marked may not only be objectionable when

in their best condition, but are liable to become more so as they become sharper, from gradually yielding to the tendency of the train to go towards the outside of the curve.

The starting point for measuring the ordinates is optional and may be at either end of the curve.   Place one end of the string upon the rail where the curve begins, and, having measured and marked the middle ordinate upon the rail, move up and place the same end of the string upon the rail at the chalk mark and measure the new ordinate, and thus proceed around the curve.   It will take three men to do this, one at each end of the string and one at the middle to measure and mark the ordinates.

This method of lining can be used in all cases, and particularly where the track has been raised or cross-ties renewed, and it is the desire to have good line without an instrument.   It is recommended, also, to show up any bad swings in curves which are not perceptible to the eye, and particularly those at the beginning of the curve, which are caused by the curve being too sharp at that point.

One of the reasons such "kinks" are permitted to remain in main-track curves so long is, that foremen, as a rule, are averse to throwing the track wherever it is necessary to cut the rails to do so. Sometimes, also, being under the impression that their curves are nearly right, they hesitate to disturb them much, fearing that they may be made worse rather than better, or that such a re-lining may give tnem too much extra work.

This fear need not exist so long as the track is thrown uniformly and nearly equal ordinates are obtained. Whatever distance the track should be moved to give it good line, whether it be one inch or one foot, although it may make a little extra work, the sooner it is so moved the better, provided no better reasons exist for not doing so than those just given.

On a warm day, on account of expansion, it is difficult to throw the track towards the inside of a curve, hence it is the practice to throw it towards the high side when re-lining, and the effect is to be seen at the ends, the curve being outside of the tangent, and when it is so, it is the endeavor to hide this defect in the alignment by throwing out the tangent, and, as a result, both the curve and the tangent are distorted.

It is only necessary to go some distance upon the tangent to see the effect of such work. When near the end, the curve should be thrown in and flattened and the rails cut, should it be necessary to do so, so as in no case to have the end of the curve outside of the tangent.

10

It is, likewise, the practice to throw towards the outside to remove a sharp place. This should not be done so generally, as a defect of this kind can be corrected better by throwing the track toward the inside.

Where a point like this cannot be remedied in this manner, the rails should be cut so that the track can be re-lined and remain where it is placed after re-lining.

In lining by ordinates, the detail of the line should be gone over carefully and all the little kinks taken out before the ordinates are measured the second time.

There are other methods of lining a curve, but they are all more or less elaborate or complicated, and depend very much upon the surface of the adjacent land being level and favorable to sight and measurement.

What the trackman needs is to know how to detect and remove sharp and flat places in his curves, and to change gradually from one compound to another. All this can be done most easily by the method just given.

It is not to be supposed that only a 62-foot string can be used. One of any reasonable length will do just as well. The reason one 62 feet long is recommended is that it is a good length, a short one giving too small an ordinate for comparison, and because it is that length by which the foreman can most easily obtain the degree of curvature, and, consequently, with which he is likely to be most familiar. A string of any length between 30 and 100 feet will do, there being no necessity for confining to any particular length.

What sometimes appears to be bad alignment in a curve is due to a depression in the grade or surface of the track extending for several rail lengths. In raising track, it is sometimes raised too much and a "hump" is the result, and in running over it to hide it, the grade is not maintained, and a "hole" in the grade is the result, which shows itself more in the alignment than in the surface. When attention is called to it, it is invariably suggested to "throw the curve to line" to remedy it. This is wrong—the depression should first be raised.

THE ELEVATION OF CURVES.

It is the general supposition that wherever there is curvature there should also be elevation; that the mere fact of the existence of curvature implies the necessity of a corresponding elevation, but this is erroneous. Because a curve, whether it is a main-track or a siding curve, happens to be of say 4, 6, or any other degree of curvature, it does not follow that for that reason alone it should have a corresponding amount of elevation in inches, or, it may be, have any elevation at all.

However, the rule so generally used of a certain amount of elevation for each degree of curvature may be taken as a safe guide, so long as the total amount does not exceed 7 inches; but, as elevation is for speed rather than for curvature, any inflexible rule of 1 inch, ½ inch, or any other fraction of an inch per degree, whether it is more or less than 1 inch, cannot always be used to advantage nor applied to various rates of speed, degrees of curvature, grades and other governing conditions to be met in railroad operation.

For example: On a double-track road, where there is a grade of say 50 to 100 feet per mile, the elevation of the curve of the ascending track should not be as much as that of the descending track; and, in case of a curve upon a summit, the amount of elevation should be less than that of the same degree of curvature of a comparatively level track.

On a single track there can be no such provision made for direction as can be done on double track, and the proper way is to be governed in elevating by the amount and character of the business which predominates, and assume a safe average rate of elevation for a comparatively high speed, so as to accommodate freight and passenger trains in both directions. An elevation of $\frac{3}{4}$, $\frac{7}{8}$, or 1 inch per degree will do this, it being merely a matter of opinion as to which of these rates is preferable.

Where the traffic is almost exclusively freight, there being only a few comparatively fast passenger trains, there need not be so much elevation as where the passenger business is considerable and speed consequently greater. Three-fourths of an inch per degree is a good elevation for such conditions.

But where the freight and passenger business are of about equal importance, although the passenger trains may attain a high rate of speed, a rate of elevation should be adopted which will take them at high speed, and, at the same time, retard as little as possible the movement of the freight trains at a comparatively low speed.

The extremes of practical elevation, therefore, are about $1\frac{1}{2}$ inches per degree for the highest and $\frac{1}{4}$ inch per degree for the lowest. By experience, it will be found that for heavy freight and fast passenger trains nothing less than 1 inch per degree should be used, and that amount is recommended so long as the total elevation does not exceed $6\frac{1}{2}$ or 7 inches, which is as much elevation as should ever be put in any curve.

Unless the speed is very low, $\frac{1}{2}$ inch per degree is rather too low a rate, for the reason that, although for a short time after a curve has been put up this elevation will remain, after a while, however, particularly with a poor quality of ballast and poor road-bed, the high side of the curve is to be expected to settle, and the small amount of elevation, which at first appeared to be sufficient, disappears in places and the riding of the curve is consequently very bad. A higher rate of elevation would allow the curve to settle and yet better preserve the agreeable and safe riding of the train and the good alignment of the curve.

High spots in the low rail or low spots in the high rail make very bad riding track, there not being a sufficient total elevation to counteract the increased tendency at high speed to go towards the outside of the curve, and such places produce corresponding defects in the alignment, which, in turn, contribute to destroy the elevation.

Three-quarters of an inch per degree is, therefore, recommended in preference to $\frac{1}{2}$ inch as a minimum elevation for low speed. However, if not much elevation is desired or required, $\frac{1}{2}$ inch per degree, for a speed of say 30 miles per hour, is very good.

Having a certain amount of elevation per degree is not so much an object to be attained, provided it is not unreasonably high or low, as the manner in which the curve is elevated. The quality of the work of the foreman, therefore, enters as largely into the consideration of this question as a precise amount of elevation per degree of curvature.

The mistake is not infrequently made of assigning either insufficient or excessive elevation as the cause of a curve riding badly, when the real cause is more likely to be from a lack of uniformity in the elevation, for which the foreman alone is responsible, and which is often not thought of when expressing an opinion as to the reason a curve does not ride well.

So long as both rails, parallel and perfect as to alignment, are put up and maintained uniformly as to elevation, the curve will ride well, whether the elevation is $\frac{1}{2}$ or 1 inch per degree, provided the speed is not excessive.

The quality of the work of the trackman is, therefore, of as much importance, if not more, than simply the indiscriminate observing of a certain amount per degree.

One and a half inches per degree is an excessive and exceptional elevation and should not be used in curves above 2 or 3 degrees, because that rate is for a speed of 70 or more miles per hour, which, as a rule, is impracticable where the curvature is more than 3 degrees.

Curves of 2 degrees and less sometimes require more elevation in proportion than sharper ones, as upon them as high a rate of speed can be attained as can be upon a straight line, or higher than that upon sharper curves. As much as 2 inches per degree in a 1 or 2-degree curve may, perhaps, be admissible for very high speed, but the conditions which require so much must be exceptional and not imaginary.

A long, light curve of say 1 degree is difficult for the trackmen to line accurately, and is, therefore, liable to have in it places where the curvature may have been increased, in consequence, to

2 or more degrees, which makes the curve seem to require a corresponding higher elevation. This is often assigned as the reason more elevation should be given a curve than the rule gives it.

The necessity of such an increase is local, and if the curve were properly lined this necessity would probably be removed and the curve elevated at a less rate. To use a rule of a certain amount of elevation per degree presupposes that the foreman knows what is the degree of curvature of all the curves on his section, and, also, where the points of his compound curves are, if he has any curves of this kind.

As a general thing, this information is not possessed by him, and if he is not able to obtain it for himself, even approximately, the elevating he does is liable to be largely guesswork, and particularly so if any of his curves are compounds.

Before he attempts to do any elevating whatever he should first ascertain what is the degree of the curve he intends to elevate, and, having done that, then decide upon the amount of elevation per degree which may be considered necessary. This amount of elevation should depend upon the rate of speed, not upon the amount of curvature. That is, if it is possible to attain a speed of only about 30 miles an hour, the elevation should be at the rate of about

½ inch per degree. If, however, as much as 60 miles an hour, or more, is the usual rather than an unusual speed, then the elevation should be at the rate of not less than 1 inch per degree. The limits in the amount of elevation should be between ½ and 1¼ inches, according to the conditions mentioned on the preceding pages.

It is not to be inferred that each curve on a section may have a different elevation per degree. A suitable rate of elevation, from ½ to 1¼ inches per degree, should be adopted for the whole road, and any variation from it should be on account of grades, double track or importance of the amount or character of traffic, or some other good reason.

Upon some single-track curves the fastest speed may be only about 30 miles an hour in one direction, while in the other it may be 45 or 50, or perhaps more. The proper elevation for them would be either ¾ or ⅞ inch per degree, not exceeding a total of 6½ inches. This would take the fast trains safely and, at the same time, not retard the slow ones.

In the following table are given the elevations, at different rates of speed, for curves to 12 degrees for speeds from 10 to 70 miles an hour.

TABLE No. 36.

DEGREE OF CURVE.	ELEVATION FOR DIFFERENT SPEEDS IN MILES PER HOUR.							
	70	60	55	50	40	30	20	10
	In.	In.	In.	In.	In.	In.	In.	In.
1	1¼	1	⅞	¾	⅝	½	0	0
2	2½	2	1¾	1½	1¼	1	¾	0
3	3¾	3	2⅝	2¼	1⅞	1½	1	½
4	5	4	3½	3	2½	2	1¼	¾
5	6¼	5	4⅜	3¾	3⅛	2½	1½	1
6	6½	6	5¼	4½	3¾	3	2	1¼
7	..	6½	6⅛	5¼	4⅜	3½	2½	1½
8	..	..	6½	6	5	4	3	1¾
9	..	..	..	6½	5⅝	4½	3½	2
10	..	..	..	..	6¼	5	4	2¼
11	..	..	..	..	..	6	4½	2½
12	..	..	..	..	..	..	5	3

What should be the elevation of a 4-degree curve for a speed not exceeding 40 miles per hour? Two and one-half inches, which we find under 40 and opposite 4 degrees. What should it be for the same curve at 60 miles an hour? Four inches. What should it be for an 8-degree curve for 30 miles an hour? Four inches. What for the same curve at 60 miles an hour? Not more than 6½ inches, because a speed of 60 miles an hour is not practicable upon an 8-degree curve, and, therefore, it should not have more than the maximum for any curve, or about 6½ inches.

Another way of ascertaining what the elevation of any curve should be, according to the speed, is, by considering the middle ordinate of a chord of varying length as being equal to the total elevation, the string or chord being long or short as the speed is high or low. This ordinate will be equal to what the elevation should be, not exceeding 6½ or 7 inches, for any degree of curvature, the string being applied in exactly the same manner as explained on page 133 to find the degree of curvature. This ·is a practical and a correct method, and does not depend upon the trackman knowing anything in regard to what the degree of his curves may be.

It is only necessary for him to know what length of string or chord will give the ordinate corresponding to the proper amount of elevation. For example: To elevate at the rate of 1 inch per degree, he should use a string 62 feet long; for ½ inch per degree, a string 44 feet long.

The following is a table of middle ordinates corresponding to the proper elevation of curves to 10 degrees for speeds to 75 miles per hour:—

TABLE No. 37.

MIDDLE ORDINATES FOR ELEVATING.

MILES PER HOUR.	LENGTH OF STRING.	ELEVATION FOR DEGREES OF CURVATURE.									
		1°	2°	3°	4°	5°	6°	7°	8°	9°	10°
	Feet.	In.	In.	In.	In.	In.	In.	In.	In.	In.	In.
20	31	¼	½	¾	1	1¼	1½	1¾	2	2¼	2½
25	38	⅜	¾	1⅛	1½	1⅞	2¼	2⅝	3	3⅜	3¾
30	44	½	1	1½	2	2½	3	3½	4	4½	5
40	49	⅝	1¼	1⅞	2½	3⅛	3¾	4⅜	5	5⅝	6¼
50	53	¾	1½	2¼	3	3¾	4½	5¼	6	6½	. .
55	58	⅞	1¾	2⅝	3½	4⅜	5¼	6⅛	6	. .	. .
60	62	1	2	3	4	5	6	6½	. .	. .	. .
65	66	1⅛	2¼	3⅜	4½	5⅝	6	. .	. .	. .	. .
70	69	1¼	2½	3¾	5	6¼	. .	. .	. .	. .	. .
75	76	1½	3	4½	6	. .	. .	. .	. .	. .	. .

To use this table and method it is not necessary to know the degree of curvature.

Suppose it is desired to elevate a 1-degree curve at the rate of ½ inch per degree. In the third column, under 1 degree, ½ inch is found opposite 44 feet; 44 feet, therefore, is the length of the chord or string whose middle ordinate in a 1-degree curve is ½ inch.

Apply the string as directed on page 133, and elevate the curve as much as the ordinate measures.

If the curve is 5 degrees, at the same rate and curvature the ordinate is 2½ inches and the elevation is 2½ inches. This is found under 5 degrees and opposite 44 feet.

Upon the basis of 1 inch per degree, the length of the string is 62 feet; the ordinate and elevation of a 5-degree curve is, therefore, 5 inches.

But in case the degree of the curve is not known, what is the length of a string which would give a suitable elevation for a speed of 60 miles an hour? In the second column, opposite a speed of 60 miles, 62 feet is found to be the length of the string or cord which should be applied to the curve, without regard to what its degree of curvature may be, and its middle ordinate measured. Whatever this ordinate is should be used as the elevation, provided it does not exceed 6½ or 7 inches.

For 20 miles an hour, a string 31 feet long will give 2 inches elevation on an 8-degree curve, and one 53 feet long will give an elevation of 3 inches on a 4-degree curve for a speed of 50 miles an hour.

In every case the middle ordinate will indicate the elevation. Sixty miles an hour is not an extraordinary speed, and, if this rate is ever attained, a string not less than 62 feet long should be used in elevating, but in exceeding that length be sure that the increased length is necessary, and rarely, if ever, exceed 69 feet,

The string should be stretched tight and carefully measured and knotted at each end to show its length; also, a large knot should be made exactly midway between the knot at the ends, to mark the middle point at which the ordinate is to be measured. This middle knot should be made visible by wrapping or tying with red thread or yarn. Apply the string as directed, moving up either its half or whole length, as may be desired, and elevate accordingly.

A word of caution is necessary just here. As it is almost impossible to line a curve so perfectly by the eye that all the ordinates will be equal, an elevation equal to each ordinate should not be used at each point, unless they are all nearly equal or uniform.

This mistake is sometimes made, and, as a result, there is uniformity in neither line nor surface. An ordinate suitable to the elevation at all the points should be selected and the curve elevated accordingly.

All the ordinates of the curve should first be measured as directed, and the curve lined again and again until it is uniform; then apply the string, the length to be taken from Table No. 37, and make the elevation equal to the ordinates which are nearest uniform.

If there is a decided difference in the ordinates, there is a lack of uniformity in the alignment, and if the sharp places cannot be taken out, the elevation should gradually increase or decrease so as to avoid an abrupt change in the elevation at those points.

Before any elevating at all is done, the curve should be carefully lined and made uniform, the grade rail being in perfect surface and free from irregularities.

" Swings," that is, sharp places in the curve, without a corresponding elevation, may be easily found by the trackmen by means of the string, and can be taken out by throwing the curve slightly in or out, as may be necessary, until the ordinates are more uniform.

When a curve rides badly, before doing anything to the elevation to remedy it, make a test of its alignment with the string, and, when it has been corrected, then attend to the elevation, but not, as a usual thing, before doing so, unless it is evident at once that the cause is due to the elevation and not to the alignment.

Look out for sharp places at the ends of curves, where there is insufficient elevation.

THE APPROACH OF CURVES.

The "Approach," "Run-off," or "Easement" of a curve are equivalent expressions of the manner of going upon or off a curve. The method most generally used by trackmen is that of carrying the elevation of the curve out upon the tangent at the rate of about ½ inch to every 30-foot rail.

When this is done, the inside rail of the curve is assumed to be the grade rail—that is, it is assumed to conform to the grade line of the track, and it is not affected by the elevation of the curve.

Sometimes in elevating, the grade line is considered as being in the centre of the track, and the elevation, obtained by raising the outside rail of the curve one-half the required elevation and depressing, or what is equivalent to depressing, the inside rail the same amount.

Sometimes the outside rail is regarded as being the grade rail, and, in that case, the inside rail is depressed the full amount of the elevation. These last two methods are, however, the exceptions.

By depressing, it is not meant that the track

must be dug down and the solid road-bed disturbed. It means that both rails should be so raised that when the elevating is done the grade line will be either the high rail or the centre of the track. This may necessitate raising a part of the straight line at each end of the curve sufficiently to change the grade line to either rail or to the centre of the track, as may be desired.

It is assumed, generally, that exactly at its begining (P. C.) and ending (P. T.) the curve should have its full elevation, the rail tangent to the high side of the curve being raised gradually from the perfect level of the tangent and attaining the full elevation exactly at the beginning (P. C.) of the curve.

The length of the approach will, therefore, depend upon the amount of elevation for each 30-foot rail, the extremes of which are generally $\frac{1}{2}$ inch as the least and 1 inch as the greatest.

In Table No. 38 is given the length of the approach, in feet, for elevating at the rate of $\frac{1}{2}$, $\frac{5}{8}$, $\frac{3}{4}$, and 1 inch for every 30-foot rail, for elevations from 1 to 7 inches, 7 inches being the maximum practicable elevation for more than 7 degrees curvature.

TABLE No. 38.

ELEVATION OF CURVE.	LENGTH OF APPROACH.			
	½ Inch.	⅝ Inch.	¾ Inch.	1 Inch.
Inches.	Feet.	Feet.	Feet.	Feet.
1	60	48	40	30
2	120	96	80	60
3	180	144	120	90
4	240	192	160	120
5	300	240	200	150
6	360	288	240	180
7	420	336	280	210

In explanation of this table: What would be the length of the elevation of the straight line or the approach of a curve having 4 inches elevation and rising ¾ inch for each 30-foot rail?

In the table the answer is found to be 160 feet, or about 5 rail lengths. Measure this distance from the point of the curve, and, beginning with a perfect level, raise the rail which is tangent to the high side of the curve, at the rate of ¾ inch per 30-foot rail.

In 160 feet, or about 5 rail lengths, the full elevation of 4 inches should be attained.

If the outside, instead of the inside, rail is assumed to be the grade rail, the approach will be the same, both as to length and elevation per rail length, just as if the low rail was the grade rail.

If the grade line is in the centre of the track, the approach will be the same as to length, but the high rail will be raised and the low rail depressed one-half of $\frac{3}{4}$ of an inch, or three-eighths of an inch, for every 30-foot rail.

The same is true of any other elevation per rail length. Whether the approach should be long or short is a matter of opinion, there being advocates of both ways; but, from experience, it is found that a long and very gradual approach of say $\frac{1}{2}$ inch per 30-foot rail is undesirable, on account of the difficulty to keep it in proper surface, as well, also, because it does not always impart the most agreeable motion to the train, the length of time the car is out of level being considerable.

Upon the other hand, a short approach of 1 inch per 30-foot rail is objectionable on account of its tendency to abruptness. So, to avoid either extremes, $\frac{5}{8}$ or $\frac{3}{4}$ inch is rather to be preferred.

But, although the practice of beginning the elevation upon the straight line does very well, it is not the best way of going upon a curve, and particularly so in the case of curves of 4 degrees and more.

The true principle of the approach is rather, that wherever there is elevation there should likewise be curvature; and, although it is intended by raising the tangent to the full elevation at the beginning of the curve, to enable the train to more easily change its direction from the straight line to the curved, it only partially accomplishes what is desired, and the objectionable lurch is not obviated, but is still more evident as the curvature increases.

In carrying out this idea of curvature where there is elevation, the correct approach is obtained by curving the tangent and flattening the end of the curve slightly in such a manner that the change from the tangent to the curve is made gradually, the curvature beginning light, say 1 degree for about the first 50 feet, 2 degrees for the second 50 feet, and 3 degrees for the third 50 feet, and so on, the elevation also increasing correspondingly to the curvature. This makes the approach a series of short compounded curves, and, practically, is equivalent to what is called a transition curve, that is, one having a rapidly changing radius or increasing curvature for a short distance between the tangent and the full degree of the curve.

The line of this compounded approach is difficult to obtain without the use of an instrument, but only partial success, practically, upon the part of the trackman, by his eye and by

using the string for the middle ordinate, will
give a better approach in the case of sharp curvature than that obtained by simply elevating the
tangent.

If all curves at the ends were in correct alignment, it would not be difficult to give offset distances, at points about 50 feet apart, to which the
end of the curve could be thrown to make this
gradually increasing approach, but, as they are
invariably more or less out of line, it is impossible
to give anything which would not be subject to
the peculiar conditions of each individual curve,
and, therefore, could not be reliable.

There are what are known as spiral curves,
easement curves, elastic curves, &c., all of them
being modifications of the end of the curve,
equivalent to this curved approach, but they are
all more or less complicated theoretically, expen-
sive, difficult to maintain and require an engineer with an instrument to give their line, so
that, from a practical point of view, they are of
little use to the trackman.

All that is necessary to improve the approach
of any curve ought to be so simple that it can
be done by the foreman himself.

The use of the string, which is recommended
for lining and elevating, is also recommended
to assist the trackman in obtaining the line and

elevation of the approach, and should be used in the same manner.

As a rule, the ends of curves are much out of line, it not being rare to find a 4-degree curve increased to 6 or 7 degrees at the ends.

This is the accumulating result of the bad practice of always moving the track towards the high side and continuing the lining out upon the tangent for a short distance. The ends of curves are thus made too sharp and the tangent is likewise distorted. This is apparent, not by standing upon the end of the curve and looking in the direction of the tangent, but by standing upon the tangent as far as possible from the curve and looking towards the curve. Where this is the case, it should be corrected at once.

Although such defects in the alignment may be known to the foreman, they are often long permitted to remain because he does not wish to cut the rails to correct them, which, generally, has to be done.

But, as a general thing, he is not aware of the real cause of the curve being bad, and endeavors by going over or changing the elevation to remedy it.

Whenever there is a lurch or bad swing at the beginning or end of a curve, the first thing to be done should be to measure the ordinates and see if the curve is in correct line at the ends. If the ordinates at the ends are greater than those further around the curve, it indicates that the curve is sharper there than it should be, and the track should be thrown towards the low side, cutting the rails, if necessary; and not only should it be thrown until the original, or correct, curvature is restored, but it should be flattened still more and the change made gradually from the straight line to the curve by means of a gradually increasing curve. It will be necessary to go back upon the tangent from 50 to 100 feet, according to the degree of the curve, to do this.

Wherever the end of the curve appears to be sharp, or outside of the line of the tangent, it will invariably be found to be so, and it should at once be corrected, going to considerable trouble, if necessary, to do it.

When the flattening is done, the curved approach should be elevated an amount corresponding to the increasing curvature, rising gradually from the level of the tangent to the full elevation of the curve, just as the alignment gradually changes from a straight line to the full curvature in a certain number of feet.

The natural inquiry is, how much should the curve be thrown at the end to make this gradually increasing approach ?

It is possible to give this only approximately, as it will depend upon how much the curve is out of line at the end and also upon finding the exact beginning or end of the curve, and any distances or offsets given could be used only when the curve is in correct alignment; so, whatever is accomplished will have to be done by the trackman in his own practical way. But for the purpose of assisting him, in Table No. 39 are given some approximate distances, which may be used as offsets to be measured from either rail towards the inside of the curve, to show to about what extent the end of the curve should be moved, provided it is already in good alignment. But as curves are invariably out of line, not too much dependence should be placed upon the figures in this table, as they are only intended for curves already in true alignment, and also where the ends (P. C. and P. T.) are marked or when they are correctly assumed.

No curve or flattened approach is necessary unless the curvature is 4 degrees or more. Whenever a 3-degree curve, or less, seems to require an elasticated, or flattened, approach it is evident that the ends are badly out of line, and if thrown to their correct line and elevated in the usual way, and kept in that condition, the curve has all that is necessary, provided, of course, the work of the trackman is carefully done. In other words, regular or compound curves to 3 degrees require no flattening.

The following is a table of approximate off-set distances which may be used for lining approaches:—

TABLE No. 39.

DEGREE.	OFFSETS AT 50 FEET POINTS ON CURVE.									
	100 Feet.	50 Feet.	P. C. o.	50 Feet.	100 Feet.	150 Feet.	200 Feet.	250 Feet.	300 Feet.	350 Feet.
	In.	In.	In.	In.	In.	In.	In.	In.	In.	In.
4	. .	. .	1	1½	1	. .	. .	. .	. .	. .
4½	. .	. .	1	2	2	. .	. .	. .	. .	. .
5	. .	. .	1½	2½	2½	1½	. .	. .	. .	. .
5½	.	½	2	3	3	2½	. .	. .	. .	. .
6	. .	1	2½	4½	4½	3½	2½	. .	. .	. .
6½	. .	1½	3½	5½	6	5½	4	2½	. .	. .
7	½	2	4½	6	7	6	5	3½	. .	. .
7½	1	2	5	7½	8½	8	6	4½	3	. .
8	1	3	6½	9	10½	10	8½	6½	4½	2

To use this table, assume, as nearly as possible, where the curve begins, and mark this point as the beginning (P. C.), and measure 50-foot distances around the curve as far as may be necessary, making a chalk mark upon the base of the rail at each 50-foot point. Return to the beginning (P. C.) and measure in the direction of the straight line 50 or 100 feet, according to the degree of curvature.

Measure the offset distance at each point, taken from the table, from the inside base of the rail to the top of a stake previously driven into the ballast, level with the top of the cross-tie, and mark it upon the top. Throw the track so that the edge of the base of the rail is exactly over the mark in the top of the stake and line between the points, and the approach, if not exactly right, should be something near what is desired, provided the end of the curve was in its true or good alignment before flattened in this manner.

One of the objections to flattening the ends of a curve is, that the foreman is liable to make the approach too flat, and, as a result, increase the curvature too much where it joins the full degree of the curve.

There is a natural slight increase in the curvature where the approach blends into or is lost in the full curvature, which is of no consequence practically, but if it is still more increased by the beginning of the approach being too flat, it becomes very objectionable, and what has been gained at the beginning of the curve is thus lost further upon it.

If the curve cannot be flattened enough by using the offsets in Table No. 39, it will likely be found that it is because it is already too sharp at the end.

TO LINE AND ELEVATE A REVERSE CURVE.

Very often what is supposed to be a reverse curve is not a true reverse curve at all. As explained on page 129, a reverse curve reverses at a point, there being no straight line whatever between the curves forming it. However, any two curves in opposite directions, having between them a short tangent of about 50 or 100 feet, do form what is practically a reverse curve, and may be treated as such in lining and elevating.

Such a piece of straight line enables the reverse to be lined and elevated more easily than if it were a genuine reverse, which, to be improved easily, should have, where the reversing point is supposed to be, not a straight line, but a flattening of both curves slightly from the reversing point, so as to make the curvature increase gradually, as is done in the approach of a curve.

In every case of lining a genuine, or what may be practically a reverse curve, the track should always be thrown or lined towards the inside of the curve, making the end of the curve upon each side of the reversing point similar to the approach of a curve.

No practical or reliable method can be given for accomplishing this perfectly; it will have to be done by the eye and the exercise of good judgment by the foreman.

When the reverse has been flattened after the manner of the approach, and appears to be satisfactory, then measure the middle ordinates, and if they increase with any degree of regularity it is fair to presume that the end of the curve is in fairly good line.

The only difference between lining the approach of a regular curve and that of a reverse curve is, that in the former the curvature can be begun a reasonable distance out upon the tangent, whereas in the latter, particularly if it is a genuine reverse, the end of the curve must be flattened within itself. The result is, of course, a slight increase, theoretically, in the curvature further upon the curve, but it does not amount to much practically, and can be distributed in lining so as not to affect the riding of the train.

The elevating of a reverse curve is done exactly in the same manner as the approach of a curve is elevated, viz., by using the middle ordinate of a string or chord.

The middle ordinates should be measured, and a corresponding amount of elevation used, provided the ordinates increase regularly from nothing to the full curvature, just as in an ordinary approach the elevation increases correspondingly with the curvature, that is, from nothing to the full elevation.

At a point midway between the two curves, whether it is the point of reverse curvature or the middle of a short straight line, both rails should be made perfectly level. If the total elevation of the curve is, say 4 inches, then from this level point to where the full elevation is reached, the elevation should increase to 4 inches, at the same rate and in the same distance that the curvature increases from nothing to the full curvature, whatever it may be.

The Roadmaster and Foreman

THE AMERICAN RAILWAY TRACK JOURNAL.

TENTH YEAR.

PENNSYLVANIA RAILWAY.

"Inclosed you will find $1.00 as a subscription to THE ROADMASTER AND FOREMAN. I notice a great many articles of interest from different foremen and other writers. I like your paper very much, and think it should be in the hands of every foreman."—S. S. KUHN, S. F.

C., R. I. & P. RAILWAY.

"I have been reading your valuable journal one year, and while I am in the track service will continue to do so, for saying it is a valuable paper is not doing it justice. Every trackman in America should take it."—W. J. GIST, S. F.

NORTHERN PACIFIC AND MANITOBA RY.

"I am in receipt of my first copy of THE ROADMASTER AND FOREMAN, and think it is the best track journal I have ever read. I am only sorry I did not get it long ago, but as long as I remain in the track service I will not be without it. It is both interesting and instructive; just what every foreman should have."—J. MCPHAIL, S. F.

UNION PACIFIC RAILWAY.

"After carefully reading several copies of your journal, handed me by a friend, will say that it is the strongest lever of light and knowledge that has ever been presented to trackmen. It is the very thing we need to bring about a system of ideas and work. Any man who wishes to follow railroading and wants advancement and improvement should subscribe for THE ROADMASTER AND FOREMAN or be classed as a drone if he does not."—JOHN MARCUS, S. F.

Subscription Price, $1.00 Per Year.

Address **Roadmaster and Foreman,** 91 & 93 Jefferson St., Chicago.